D1603546

Twenty-Four Years a Cowboy and Ranchman in Southern Texas and Old Mexico

Desperate Fights with the Indians and the Mexicans

by Will Hale

THE NARRATIVE PRESS

TRUE FIRST PERSON ACCOUNTS OF HIGH ADVENTURE

The Narrative Press
P.O. Box 2487, Santa Barbara, California 93120 U.S.A.
Telephone: (805) 884-0160 Web: www.narrativepress.com

ISBN 1-58976-100-6 (Paperback)
ISBN 1-58976-101-4 (eBook)

Produced in the United States of America

TABLE OF CONTENTS

Chapter 1

MY START.

My first writing is about the Mexican War. Being a very small boy my recollections of what happened during the war are very meager, my information coming mainly from hearing other people talk on the subject. I will attempt to write what little I know and to give some history dates.

My father, Henry Hale, was an appointed captain under Taylor, or with him, rather. The part that was not in the battle, the part that was out of danger – old Texas – had been claimed as Spanish American possessions. The Spanish had settled in Texas as early as 1715. When the United States purchased Louisiana from France, the Americans claimed Texas as part of that purchase, but the United States gave up all claims when she purchased Florida from Spain in 1819. So Texas came under the Spanish government until the year of 1821. Mexico and Texas declared themselves independent of Spain, after which a large immigration moved to Texas from various nations. Texas remained under the Mexican government about fourteen years, or until the year of 1835. During this year the people refused to obey the Mexican laws and when the Mexican president tried to force them into submission it caused a war that lasted during the years of 1835 and 1836.

The Mexican army got badly whipped in the Battle of San Jacinto and the Mexican president was taken prisoner. After Texas whipped Mexico she put up a government of her own, Sam Houston, president. A very short while after Texas asked to be annexed to the United States. This was pro-posed in 1844. The population was at this time about 1,600,000. Old Mexico claimed Texas as part of her territories and the western part was in dispute. Texas claimed her country reached west-ward to the Rio Grande; Mexico claimed different, so the Greasers made preparations to defend what they called their rights.

In the summer of 1845, Taylor was ordered to the disputed territory and in the spring moved in on the Rio Grande, opposite Matamoros and at this place built Fort Brown. Taylor moved most of his army to Point Isabel. Soon after the Mexicans attacked Fort Brown, but met defeat when Taylor came from Point Isabel and worked on them a while. On the seventh of October, Taylor moved on the Mexicans at Palo Alto and on the eighth defeated an army of 6,000, killing and wounding about 2,000 men.

The scouts had some trouble with the Mexican scouts, the Mexicans gaining nothing.

Chapter 2

BATTLE OF RESACA DE PALMA.

This was the next battle. The Mexicans retreated leaving over 1,000 killed and wounded. There was no trouble after this except with the scouts. General Taylor crossed the Rio Grande and captured Matamoros. The news of the capture of Thornton's men by the Mexicans reached Washington and caused great excitement throughout the United States.

Congress declared war between the United States and Mexico and prepared to raise an army, which was easily done, as volunteers came forward in great numbers. Congress planned the campaign, and divided the volunteers into two sections. Kearney was to invade the Spanish possessions of New Mexico and California and conquer that part. Another under General Wool was to invade and operate in the northern part of Old Mexico and conquer Chihuahua and Taylor was to still hold the line of the Rio Grande and work on the Mexicans from that part of the country; Taylor did nothing but get his men ready for the coming battles. He was reinforced during the summer at Matamoros, and in September, 1846, he made preparations. The scouts had some trouble and a few were killed.

I wanted father to leave the army, but he only laughed at me and told me they might want me out next time with the scouts. Next day there went out from the army about 140. They had some shooting to do, but ran the Mexican scouts into the town of Monterrey and got a good view of the Mexican army. They rode back and informed Taylor that they had ran the Mexicans in and got a good view of their army and said they believed there were over 9,000.

On September 20, 1846, Taylor moved against Monterrey. The first day's battle and siege was very destructive to the Mexican army. After four days of siege and assault Monterrey surrendered. Taylor remained at Monterrey many days resting and recruiting his army, after which he moved and took Saltillo, some time in October. Taylor had peaceable possession of the Rio Grande – at least he thought so. We will see later. Taylor sent some Mexicans who were serving under him to go in and learn if the enemy would make an attempt to take him by surprise, and let him know. Most of Taylor's army was marched to help General Scott, who was to make an invasion of Mexico by the way of Vera Cruz.

Taylor's army was reduced to a great extent from what it was before. We still stayed in camp and the Mexican president, the old reprobate, learned this and collected his forces together, which consisted of over 20,000 men. The spies informed Taylor of this and said that the Mexican president was making preparations to capture his army and had collected thousands of men. The next one came in and told him the other got drunk and told him what business he had come on, and they had taken him out and shot him. They also said Santa Ana was on his march with 20,000 or 30,000 men, but they were mistaken, for there were only 20,000. This did not alarm Taylor for he knew the proper place to stop him was in the narrow pass and give battle so the large Mexican army could not get around him. Taylor and his men got everything ready for the coming battle. The men got their firearms ready and were well prepared for the struggle.

Chapter 3

BATTLE IN THE NARROW MOUNTAIN PASS OF BUENA VISTA.

Taylor went to meet this large army and had his cannons placed so they would deal destruction to the copper-colored lads. The Mexicans arranged theirs as they came on and placed them in front. They began to fire on us before they got in range, but we were so much higher than they that the volley did us no damage. The Mexicans kept on firing; Taylor, thinking things were getting serious, ordered his men to begin to fire and Anderson, who was in front and the center, ordered his men to the cannons, which they did. The Mexicans kept up their firing but did us no harm as we were sheltered by the rocks. The Mexicans were slaughtered in great numbers by our soldiers, Taylor attempting nothing decisive but had his men stay as they were and mow down the Mexicans. As soon as the Mexicans filled up their ranks they were shot down. They began to grow impatient. Santa Ana ordered his men in front to charge, which they did, while the cannons kept on at their dreadful work. When they got pretty close the infantry fired on them two or three times, and the fire killed so many they went to the bottom of the hill. They were ordered back, but it was as before. They came back again and were defeated with great slaughter. Our guns made a dreadful havoc among them; even the wind was in our favor, it set the tall grass on fire and the smoke from the guns and the fire blew on them. They had to fight the flames as well as our men. I could see all of this from the heights. Then the Mexican president gave the order to retreat.

Our men at the cannon kept on firing on them and continued their dreadful work until the Mexicans got out of range of the guns. Santa Ana was badly defeated, his men and army were worn out from the fierce attack made by our soldiers. The victory at this place released all fear of an invasion on the Mexican side. There was seldom any battle equal to this – so large a force against such a small one. After this Taylor was at liberty to direct his whole force against Vera Cruz. Well, this is all about our part. Father was wounded before the war was over and we went to the ranch.

I will give an idea to the reader how the Mexican War closed. General Scott's army went to the City of Mexico. General Kearney conquered the Mexicans in California. General Scott's force landed at Vera Cruz and after a fearful battle captured the city and castle. From here Scott marched to the City of Mexico. The Mexican president collected an army of about 30,000 men. Scott had about 10,000.

The Mexican president put them in a pass and tried to stop Scott, like Taylor did him, but failed in this. So Scott and his men drove them out of the pass. After many bombardments and sieges Scott captured the City of Mexico. This ended the war. The treaty of peace was signed and agreed upon.

After we got back to the ranch the boys said they had had some trouble with Indians and negro soldiers, who had deserted. There were some Indians who had bothered the boys during the war and caused some trouble, for they wanted the horses of the white men. I will give an account of one killing. There being no soldiers in that part of the country the Indians tried to steal the horses from three ranches and succeeded in all but ours. At Williams' ranch they left only as many horses as needed to mount his men. Williams' men gave chase but came very near being killed for there was a large number of Indians. They killed three of his men and ran the others into camp. One Indian shot Williams with a bow and an arrow but he received only a slight wound. Getting in camp the Indians gave up the chase. Another man had a similar experience with the savages. They stole his horses one night and he followed and had a great battle, killing many of them, but gained nothing. Only three or four of his men were shot, and none were seriously injured. The men working for these stock men took a lot of horses from the Mexicans, who were afraid to do anything on account of the war with Uncle Sam. So the cowmen after supplying themselves with horses from the Mexican side could run their cattle without any trouble. But every time they got a chance at an Indian they generally put a bullet hole through him. Many an Indian bit the dust after this.

Well, I will tell how they commenced on our men. The boys saw some Indians watching our horses. Mr. Wheeler was managing father's ranch for him while he was gone. Ernest Wheeler proposed to watch the horses, Wheeler and Mills taking the first guard. Toward the last they were concealed in some bushes, when all of a sudden they saw four objects coming towards the horses. They were creeping like dogs. All at once Mills and Wheeler fired a shot each and killed the two in front. The others were shot in the same manner, and by the time the other boys got out Mills and Wheeler had their guns reloaded. Wheeler ordered the horses moved, and said there would be trouble if they or the Indians would be back after their dead. So the horses were moved and the watches were arranged differently – two instead of so many. One of the boys who was on the last watch shot at a wolf just for fun, which aroused the boys, who did not go to bed again that night.

Chapter 4

CAPTURE SOME NEGRO SOLDIERS AND ONE OF THE BOYS SHOOTS AN INDIAN, WHO WAS ACTING LIKE A HOG, SO HE COULD SCARE THE HORSES OFF, THEN STEAL THEM.

The next day all the boys but three rode out and shot a couple of buffaloes for fresh meat. They also shot at a couple of Indians who ran into a thicket. The boys knew better than to molest them in such a place, for when an Indian gets in a thicket he could kill as many men as he wants to with his bow and arrows, for when his arrows would fall short he could cut green sticks and shoot them through a man. So the boys went back to the ranch with some of their fresh meat. That evening four negroes came up and wanted supper. The boys told them all right and gave them their suppers. The boys said they had asked a great many questions and caught them in a great many lies. They relieved the negroes of their revolvers and ordered them to lie down, and tied them hand and foot and put them in front of the big blazing fire with one man at a time to watch them and gave instructions that the first man turning over would have a bullet hole through him. This talk they made had a good effect on the prisoners, for they never turned over once. Next morning two of the boys took them to Fort Brown, where they were wanted as deserters. The next day the boys rode out and looked after the cattle and shot four or five Indians. That same night a couple of the boys were watching the horses and one noticed something coming along like a hog. When it got close it began to grunt like a hog. Harden knew there was no hog any closer than Fort Brown, and was not certain what could happen. So he thought he would shoot him for luck. He took out his revolver and shot two or three times, and one or more of the boys came out to see what was the matter. He told them he had only shot a hog. On looking at it they found it to be an Indian who was making for the horses in order to scare and eventually steal them.

The boys were very watchful after this. The other ranches sent men to our ranch to help run back the Indians. So they decided to all go and give battle. The boys got everything ready and drove the Indians sixty miles up the river. They came to a large Indian camp and they thought the best thing they could do was to return, and after they came back to the ranch a large government outfit went up the river and the Indians retired and went up towards the foot of the plains. So the boys on the ranches were troubled no more during the war with the Indians.

I will relate a love story that happened during the war. George Dixon and Sam Brown fell in love with a couple of girls. One was a Mexican and the other Mexican and Spanish. The boys were not so much in love as the girls were. The boys went to see them one or more times a week. One day they went horseback riding and the girls' father got angry and also said he never liked to have American boys come to see his girls. The boys said nothing to him only went when they got ready. This began to happen often and the boys went walking with the girls after their father stopped them from taking his daughters horseback riding. This continued a long time. The girls thought there was no one like the boys. The old Mexican got so he would not look at the boys, let alone speak. The boys did not visit the girls while some branding was going on, but in a short while the work was over and the boys were at liberty to continue their attentions. They stayed all day and the old Mexican began to like them, and at one time gave them a fine dinner. The boys began to think they were one of the family and planned to take away the girls. They got so smitten with the girls that they wanted to marry them and planned a trip to Corpus Christi. One night they stole the girls and ran away with them and married them at Corpus Christi. This was unexpected to all. The father, after he had discovered the elopement, came to the ranch with blood in his eye. The boys told him the girls were not there, and after staying two or three days he was convinced. Someone told him the girls were at Corpus Christi and had married a couple of gringoes, which means American in the Mexican language. The old man wished they were dead and swore that he would kill both boys and girls. The old Mexican lost two girls, and Wheeler two men from the ranch. The old Mexican was told by another Mexican, who was a cripple and resided at Corpus Christi. The old greaser always hated the Americans and believed his girls had disgraced themselves and his family. Wheeler said they were all disgraced, the ones that married one another, and their relatives.

The cowboys got along all right but a little later got to fighting among themselves. It was all Wheeler could do to prevent killing. He said there was not enough work to keep their nerves quiet. Well, as father and I came back to the ranch everything was getting along nicely. Father had the men finish branding, for there was a lot of work to do. Branding was over in August and father had recovered from his wound about the last of August, and made preparations to send me to school. He thought I was anxious to go and he wanted me to be with other children, still he was undecided whether to send me or not. I was not anxious to go – in fact I was afraid to leave father, and begged to stay with him, but he never paid any attention to me.

It was about this time that gold was discovered in California. The people had the fever so great, they thought that gold grew on trees and all they need do was to pull it off. A great many went and found out different. A great many went from our part of the country.

When I was about eight years old and was pretty mean, father concluded to send me to school and see if the professors could learn me anything and make a smart boy of me as Henry Clay, whom the Democrat, President Polk, beat in the race in the year of 1845. Father had me go with him to Galveston, and from there sent me to New York city to attend an institute. He made preparations for my board, and also the money I needed. In September, 1848, I started to school and everything went nicely. I was boarding with a widow lady by the name of Mrs. Williams.

First three weeks went nicely, but the next week was not so nice for me and her boy, whose name was Jim Williams. So me and Jim were great chums. This is where I boarded. Because a boy by the name of Smith told a lie on another boy he was to get a whipping next day; but after they all left, me and Jim Williams hid the switches. But a brother of the Smith boy saw us and told the teacher. Next day he called me and Jim up, and what that teacher did for us was plenty. I thought he was going to wear out a thicket of switches on us. One thing I can and will say: we never hid any more switches. Then the Johnson boy, who was to get the whipping, ran off and quit school. One good thing, he whipped the Smith boy for telling on us. Me and Jim were the ones who came out damaged and there was no way for us to get even with that teacher and we were also afraid to. Mrs. Williams thought I was a great boy, but the teacher thought different.

Along in October, about the twenty-fifth, me and the Williams boy began to get over our bruises, from hiding switches, so I prepared to do something to get even with that teacher, so me and Jim held a secret meeting like a lodge of some kind, not like some lodges, for they never tell anything, and I am telling this at the last. So we had our meeting and tried to think up something that would do the teacher a damage and also have a laugh on him. Me and Jim proposed a great many things and it seemed that none of them would do, so Jim said, put a chicken in his desk. I said no, I know where there is a snake who has gone into winter quarters, and we will get him and put him in the old scoundrel's desk. So we got our plans and everything ready. The snake was secured and the snake being numb we had no trouble in securing him. The snake was one of those kind that made his home in hollow trees, when trying to get out of the cold or danger. I told Jim we would locate the teacher and you watch him, and if he comes to the schoolhouse or in sight, you want to whistle and I will crawl in the barrel in the corner. So the snake was shut up until Monday morning. School was begun as usual. It was quite a while before he went where the snake was hidden. He heard several classes and a little later went in his desk after some papers and pencils, or something else. The snake was feeling like summer time on account of the room being very warm – at least that was my opinion. The way the snake acted! As soon as the teacher opened the drawer for his pencils the snake saw the hole in his sleeve and I suppose the snake thought it was a hole in a hollow log or a tree, by the way it acted, so the snake went up his sleeve. The teacher saw it and yelled and was so badly scared he could not do anything. None of the scholars knew what was wrong, for he had them afraid to take their noses out of their books.

All at once he jumped so high that he made two or three running motions in the air, before he touched the floor. He yelled the devil had him or sent some of his angels, which was just the same, he said. The scholars thought he was going crazy. The first thing he did was to dance a clog and the next was to pull off his coat and a little later his vest. The snake was next to his body. He began to act as if he was going to pull off his shirt. And out went the boys and girls, for they thought he was a lunatic or something else. I or Jim did not know how many clothes he did shed. For I knew this was the time for me and Jim, so I says, let's us go, and we got out in a hurry. We went home and told Mrs. Williams that the teacher went crazy and went to pulling his clothes off in the schoolhouse. Mrs. Williams said it never surprised her for he was a fool to begin with, and also said he would not have far to go to go crazy. She told me and Jim to go to play, and not go back to school where the old fool was, as she called him.

It took two days to see the parents and get the children started again, so me and Jim were proud of our vacation, and said we would try and think of something else in the future. We started again to school and studied hard. The teacher knew someone had put the snake there, but thought an older boy, whom he had whipped a couple of days before, had done the work. The teacher said nothing, for he wanted to catch the guilty one. He never dreamed us little imps did the mischief. And we did not want him to, either.

Everything went along nicely until the last of November. The boy that told on me and Jim got mad at Jim because Jim would not speak to him, and he tried to whip Jim, but Jim got him down and the boy's oldest brother went to jump on Jim and did. Before he had time to do anything I hit him with a good-sized stick and laid him out. So Williams gave the other a good licking. There was nothing wrong with this only I got a whipping for trying to kill the other boy. I thought we all should get a whipping, but never said anything to the teacher about it. I thought of my whipping, having gotten more whippings than any of the other scholars, and I wished to do something mean to the teacher and get even with him. And it came so I thought I could be successful.

Just before he closed school he told the scholars that there would be one or two days he would be absent and there would be no school, and also said when those days came he would put a card on the door saying what days they would be. He also said you scholars come before I do and see the card and can go home. School was dismissed and we all went home.

I said to Jim, I will put that card there for the old man and have four days instead of two. So I studied how I would manage, and at last it came to me. I went down town and got an old negro friend of mine to put that on a card. I told him what I was going to do with it and I also told him how mean the old teacher had been to me. I asked him if he would say nothing about it. He says, "No, honey, I never will tell anyone." The card read, no school the rest of the week, and I went and put it on the schoolhouse door.

Next morning the children all came before the teacher and went home. When all had left, me and Jim tore it up and put it in the stove. So me and Williams went home and went to playing, after we had told the news, and we had a fine time. The teacher came to school and when no one came he got mad and went home. The next day he came as usual and went home.

The next day he went to see the people who were sending their children. They told him the reason. He was mad, because they had not been attending. He raised Cain and said there would be no more school until Monday. He said, the next Monday, if he could find out who did that he would whip them within an inch of their lives. So school commenced again next Monday. He made a great talk on what he would do to anyone if they were guilty of such again. School went nicely the rest of the year 1849. One time while passing his house I saw a wild cow of Parson Amos go in his small barn, so I went through the cracks and shut her up. When he went to feed his cow and horse she would run over him. So he went to the barn, thinking it strange it being closed, and when he opened the door the wild cow ran over him and knocked him down and injured his spine. This did away with school the rest of January, but when school did commence he made such a war talk that I was afraid to do anything more to him the rest of the year. He had blood in his eye and I also thought it best to do nothing, as our school was out in June.

There was nothing of importance the rest of the year, only they had a fine time the Fourth of July, 1849. We had a fine time – nice entertainments – we could not wish any better time. My father came up from the ranch to see how I was getting along and made a lot of inquiries. Mrs. Williams told father there were lots of the boys who were giving the teacher some trouble and they were so shrewd he could not find out who it was. I spent most of my time with father and the rest with Jim. Mrs. Williams told father how proud she was of me and Jim, and how many whippings me and Jim had got.

Father only smiled and said it would loosen our hides and make us grow, and therefore be a great benefit to us.

Father went home, or back to the ranch, in a few days. I wanted to go with him, but he said, "No, stay there and let that teacher learn you something." I could have told him me and Jim was about to learn the teacher something. I thought it was the best to say nothing about it, as Mrs. Williams might have a bad opinion of me, and me and Jim wanted to keep our record clear in regard to her opinion.

Chapter 5

SCHOOL COMMENCES AGAIN – THE SAME OLD TEACHER – THE PRINCIPAL AGAIN. ME AND JIM SAYS WE WILL DEAL HIM MISERY.

School began in September. So me and Jim started again. First week went along nicely, for only one boy got a whipping. One thing, it was neither I nor Jim. Another week was not so nice, for the teacher had me and Jim standing up for one hour. The cause of this was talking in school. The time I thought never would pass. It seemed like three hours instead of one, to me. Jim said it seemed like a week instead of an hour. Oh! I did get tired. I became so wearied that I would stand on one foot and then the other trying to rest my feet. At last both of my feet played out. The teacher told us to take our seats, and we did, but never spoke to one another. We planned to do something to him.

After all had left the school ground and went home, me and Jim stopped up the stove pipe, and the next day they all came and built a fire and it smoked them out. Everyone was forced to leave the house. The day was very cold, and the teacher told us to go home and he would see if he could find out what was the matter with it. He told a larger boy to stay and help him. He took the pipe down and then to pieces, and found an old shirt next to the stove. He sure got mad and said he would whip the boy that did it until he could not sit up, and says, "I would just as soon think Hale and Williams done this as not." And says, "I will make inquiries to see if they were late on the school ground or not." He made his inquiries and found out nothing. But when school commenced he called me and Jim up and asked us if we had done this. We told him no. He said he believed me and Jim done this, and if he knew for certain he would whip us for an hour. The only thing that saved me and Jim was being first-class talkers and liars also. So we got away safe and sound. We were very careful what we did after this. In fact we never did anything that was worth mentioning.

There was another boy who was terrible mean, and he got the teacher's mind off us for a few days anyway. He was always doing something, but the teacher never could catch him. He did his meanness in the room where the teacher was. The teacher put his hands over his face and this boy made a face at him. The teacher saw him and called him up and gave him a few strokes, and the boy went to his seat. So I suppose the teacher thought someone else was mean besides us.

The fourth week and the last day of the week me and Jim got smitten with a couple of girls, and they liked us about as well as we did them. Anything nice me and Jim could bring for them we did. So we bought some candy and brought it to school, and I told Jim I would ask to get a pencil and deliver the candy.

I asked the teacher and he said I could go. I got the pencil and delivered the candy and a note with it also. The teacher saw me and he jumped like a bear by my side and says, "Let me have that note and candy." And he read the note aloud, which read this way: "From your lovers, Jim and Will." He looked at me and then at Jim and says, "You little bantams, I will teach you how to love." He was so mad he looked at one time like a black bear, and at another like a silver tip, and a second later like a cinnamon. All at once the silence was broken. He says, "Come up and I will teach you how to love." So we marched up in a single file like Indians I am told.

After working on us a while with a couple of switches, he says, "There is a mark, I want to see who can reach the highest and closest to it." If we had been twelve years older we might have reached the mark, as it was we could not. So when one of us would outreach the other he would whip the other to make him come up. After whipping us quite a while he told us to take our seats, which we did without the second invitation.

He also told us, that should we need any help in our love affairs, to let him know, and he would do everything in his power to make things pleasant for us. He came very near making me and Jim over-reach ourselves.

We never had much to say to our girls next week. Me and Jim liked our girls just the same. We would go and play with them Saturdays and Sundays. We always made our trip when they called on one another, and they always told us when they did so.

On the fifteenth of October, a boy by the name of Johnson got a whipping for talking to a girl, but he never tried to make him reach anything like us. I proposed to Jim to do something mean to the old scoundrel for whipping us for giving the candy to our loved ones.

One night after our home people had gone to bed, me and Jim tied a large can to his milk cow's tail. We first went to the fence with the can, for she was against it. We took her tail and tied the can good and fast. At first she began to stir, and when she did the can began to rattle. She began to run and the can rattled like a tin shop that was turned over. Then she tore down the side of the fence and went down town, hitting the ground in high places. The teacher came out when she tore down the fence, but me and Jim were gone. We went home and went to bed. Jim laughed a week and said it was better than anything we had done before and a great deal more fun.

The teacher had a lost cow for a couple of days. His cow almost lost her senses when the dogs got after her down town and chewed on her flank a while. She lost her can, and when the teacher did get her she was badly disfigured. If it had been a little more she would have been finished for life.

The professor never made any complaint to anyone. He sent a note to Mrs. Williams asking if me and Jim were at home that night. Mrs. Williams wrote to him that we were. So the outlaws were safe again, if we did not give it away in our talk. Me and Jim took an oath to be careful. The teacher made inquiries about the Johnson boy to see whether he was at home also. So the teacher never got his scalp. After we had canned the cow Jim wanted to can everything. I am of the opinion he would have canned the teacher if he did not like to live so well.

Friday came and my girl's sister gave a party. My girl went over to the other's home to get her, and when they were both ready we were to be ready also and go with them, which we did. We could not mix with the older ones, but we got in another room and had our own fun. We enjoyed ourselves as well as the older people and part of the time better. We would look at the others from the door but never go in. It lasted until late, and we smaller ones got sleepy and me and Jim bid our girls adieu and went home and went to bed.

Monday morning we went to school and studied very hard, and learned very fast. The teacher said it was always easy for a mean scholar to learn fast, when they tried. I received a letter from father saying him and his cowboys had some trouble with the Mexican and Indian horse thieves. I will tell a little about it.

Father and twelve of his men moved their camps to a new part of the range so they could watch the cattle closer, and as soon as they had got their camp located a Mexican rode up and said they wanted all the horses they had. If they would give them up peaceably, all right; if not, they would have to fight some. Father says, "Go and tell your men we had rather fight them than give them a good word." So the Mexican rode back to his thirty Mexicans and Indians. Father told his men to get ready and they would give battle in camps or anywhere else they preferred.

Chapter 6

FIGHT WITH THE MEXICAN AND INDIAN HORSE THIEVES.

Father and his men rode out to meet them and had a terrible battle. Father and his men fell over on their horses' sides and shot them right and left. Jim Johnson got in a critical position. An Indian was about to lance him, but as rapidly as thought father put two bullet holes through the Indian. The fight went on and eighteen Mexicans and Indians were down never to rise again, and by the time the fight ended seven more had bitten the dust. They beat a retreat with bullets after them. This ended the fight, as the Mexicans and Indians concluded they wanted none of the horses.

Three of father's men were killed and two wounded. After the dead men were buried and the ones who were shot had received the best attention, father sent a man to Fort Brown to give the news to the United States soldiers. They came and ran all the Mexicans and Indians out, after having captured some.

I wrote father a letter telling him I wanted to come out and help shoot the Mexicans and Indians, but father wrote me back a letter saying it would be better shooting crawfish than Indians or Mexicans.

About the second week or some time in October or November, I meant to say, the teacher had me and Jim standing up again for being so unruly. One thing, thank goodness, it was not for hiding switches again. And another, he was not trying to make us reach anything. Boys and girls studied hard. The last part of the week some one swung a bucket over the door full of water, so when the teacher opened it he would get water all over him. But a scholar did the work before the teacher came, so the teacher never got the benefit of it. The teacher said he would just as soon believe me and Jim did this as not. Me and Jim could have told him we were too smart for that, but he would not have believed it, so we never told him. In fact we would have been afraid to, anyway. Me and Jim decided we might as well have done the work as to be accused. Jim says we will do something to the old character and it will be no failure like the water some boy prepared for him. So we planned a great many things to do unto him, but I or Jim would object. So we gave it up. I said to Jim we will watch for an opening, and when we do get a chance we will fix him.

The November school went along nicely. We never did anything to him. Our brains were not plenty, or we had not enough to get a chance at him.

Christmas came and we had a fine time. Me and Jim bought a nice lot of things for our girls and put a great many on the tree for them. We also thought of the teacher and put him up some nice negro dolls. They had a laugh on him, and me and Jim did nothing until New Year's, and then me and Jim tied some fireworks to his dog's tail, and it scorched most of the hair off his hips.

That was the last of our meanness to the teacher. During the year of 1850, we got down to work and learned very fast. During the month of May school was out. Father came up from the ranch and I was happy, too. He told me all about the ranch that would interest me. He told me how anxious the boys were to see me. He stayed until the last days of August, and he got smitten with Mrs. Williams and put in his time around the place courting her. This suited me and Jim, for I did not think anyone could fill my mother's place like Mrs. Williams could if I had another mother. They told me and Jim we could call them pa and ma. Father left for his ranch in a few days, for his men got to fighting among themselves.

Chapter 7

SCHOOL COMMENCES IN OCTOBER AGAIN WITH A NEW TEACHER WHOSE NAME WAS MOORE.

Moore was a fine man, and was good natured and mild until someone hurt his feelings. Then he was anything else but nice. At least the one whom he was mad at thought so. The first thing he did was to whip a boy for telling a lie on another. He had one rule, which was to do right. Well, I suppose I must tell what he did to me and Jim and a couple of girls whom me and Jim hated. They made an ugly face at me and Jim. We made a face back, and I threw a kiss at them. All of this was in time of study. The teacher saw us and called us up and made the girls make ugly faces and us boys do our part. We kept this up quite a while until the girls commenced to cry and us boys also. At first it was funny, but it soon got old. It was funny to the teacher and scholars, but not to us. I had the best job throwing kisses. But it soon grew wearisome. After we got to crying a while, he told us we could sit down. This hurt me and Jim worse than a whipping, yes, or even two or three. But we had to stand it. After this was over, me and Jim was very careful what we did for we had a right to be, as the teacher was a dangerous man. School went nicely from that time on. Me and Jim wanted to do something but was afraid, to his face.

Father wrote that the ranch was getting along all right and the cattle were doing fine. Some of the Comanche Indians passed through every once in a while hunting and killing buffalo. It was very seldom they would kill anyone. Two of the boys fired a few shots at four Indians one day. The Indians ran away and no one was killed. About a hundred miles above they killed a couple of buffalo hunters and scalped them.

Father wrote and said he would be up to see me in December. I thought he should have said Mrs. Williams, but I never told him so until a couple of years after. School went along nicely and the scholars learned so much faster than any of the other schools, probably because they were afraid of this teacher.

Father came up in December and I was sure proud of it. He told me I could go back to the ranch with him if I studied hard. This put me in great glee for I thought of how I could shoot Mexicans and Indians with my one-barrel revolver.

Me and Jim had our fine time as usual at the Christmas tree. Father went with Mrs. Williams and me and Jim went together, and while we were there saw our girls and went home with them. They were close to our age – almost eleven.

Father went home in January, which I disliked to see, but he went just the same. School got along fine.

There was a negro beating Mrs. Williams' hogs and cows, so I said to Jim I would fix him. I fixed my one-barrel Mexican revolver and said to Jim, "Watch me fix the yapper." While he was running them as before, he passed me and I bored it into him. He was running the cows, but never stopped until he had run about a mile. Finally he returned home and said Mrs. Williams was trying to kill him. The people did not pay any attention to it and said he should have been killed a long time ago. The bullet, being from a small gun, was taken out without much trouble. Mrs. Williams came out when the shot was fired and asked what was wrong. We told her a man ran past and fired a gun.

School got along fine until some time in February. A large boy became smitten on my girl, but she did not care for him, so the old lad thought he would take it out on me. He whipped me one day, and came very near going too far. He was so much larger that he had the advantage. The teacher whipped him, but next day he said he would whip me again. So I thought about my one-barrel revolver and took her along, and had her loaded also. Next morning he jumped on me, and not being able to stand up with him, I had my face down and he was pounding me. I tried to shoot him through the body, but made a mistake and shot him through the fleshy part of the leg, below the knee. He jumped five feet high and ran home like an antelope.

Chapter 8

A TRIP TO GALVESTON AND THEN TO THE RANCH. MY TRIP WAS VERY DISAGREEABLE AND WEARISOME.

After I had shot the boy, I ran home and got some money and ran away. I stayed out a couple of days. By chance I hid in a steam vessel and stayed around Galveston about three days or more, or until my money was getting low. Then I bought a bootblack's outfit and blackened boots and shoes, making enough money to get my meals, but could not clear enough to get a bed. A kind man who ran a confectionery store would let me sleep in a barrel, from which he had emptied the apples, and also gave me a quilt to cover myself with.

I followed my new trade for some time and often thought of Mrs. Williams' home. I thought they might kill me if I ever did go back, so I was in a bad fix, or condition, rather. I went off in a back alley and cried about an hour.

Business was dull that day and I was compelled to sell my one-barrel Mexican revolver in order to get three meals, instead of two. Times were getting gloomy in the way of boot and shoe shining. I put in my time asking if the people wanted their boots and shoes shined. One time I was yelling at the people who were passing, when up stepped a man and said, "What in the thunder are you doing here?" It was my father, who was on his way to New York. The first thing I did was to fall in his arms and commence crying. He told me to leave that outfit and come with him, and also said if I made any attempt to bring them along he would murder me. I left them and was glad to do so.

He took me to the hotel and I told him everything. He got mad and said he did not know what to make out of me, whether to leave me at my trade or make a horse thief out of me. He said he did not think I was smart enough to learn anything at school. He said he could give me to a Mexican who could teach me how to kill and steal. Father told me to stay in the room and said he would be back in a few minutes. When he did come he took me to a dry goods store and bought a fine suit of clothes for me. We stayed around Galveston eight or ten days.

We finally went back to the ranch. The boys asked father who that boy was who was with him. He told them it was a boot and shoe black, who wanted a home, whom he had picked up, or found, while in Galveston. Two of them knew me, Mr. Wheeler and Ed Johnson.

I certainly had a fine time at the ranch with the cowmen, or the cowboys, who were working under father. Father rigged me up with a Mexican saddle and gave me an Indian pony. So I had a great time horseback riding. I stayed around the ranch with father until July.

Father sold about three thousand Mexican steers to Jim Manning, who lived close to where San Marcos stands. The cattle were gathered and the wagon was gotten ready to carry the boys' beds and food. Everything was ready for us to start up the trail. I could help with the horses or do anything I wanted. Father delivered his herd all right, only losing a few head.

About the twenty-fifth of July the cattle caused a great deal of trouble. They tried to run away two or three times, but the men managed to hold them together. The trouble was caused on account of it being so dark. Father stayed up all night, thinking it was best, while I was in a tent fast asleep. Father did sleep most of the next day, and did not move camp very far.

On the day of the twenty-eighth we saw a band of Kickapoo Indians on a hunting expedition. They had their bows and arrows, and every once in a while you would see an arrow in a buffalo. There were a few along our route. The Indians acted as though they had not seen us. We were glad of that for there were only about twenty of us, while they had a band of thirty. Father and the men were not scared, but I and the fellow with the horses were, for we thought they might want our horses and then our scalps. Father delivered the cattle about the fifteenth of August.

We started back to the ranch the twenty-fifth. When we arrived there were several letters from Mrs. Williams, telling how mean a boy had treated me, and about me shooting him, and also about me running away. The letters she wrote seemed to show she was very uneasy about me. She wanted father to pay someone to search for me. She also said the boy was in bed yet, and it would be a long time before he could go on crutches. Father never answered the letters. He said he thought he had better send me back and let me finish him up, for I should not have made a cripple of him. When I cried he said he never would send his boy back for people to beat. I'm sure I felt good then. As well as I liked Jim, I never wanted to see that place again. What I wanted to do was to stay at the ranch.

After we got back father made another drive on the trail. He went close to Corpus Christi and left me at the ranch. I was a little lonesome a long time after father left. He came back in October. I stayed the winter of 1851, and also 1852, at the ranch.

In the spring of fifty-two I went with father to Austin, where some of father's relatives lived. They had some boys of my age and older. We had a fine time fishing. When we went back to the ranch father wrote Mrs. Williams that I was all right. I wrote and told her it was too bad I did not live there so father might have an excuse to come and see her.

In the fall of fifty-two, after branding was over, father went to St. Louis, Missouri, and stayed there until December, and when he came back he sent me there also. At first we went by a land route to Galveston, and from there took a steamship to New Orleans, and then to St. Louis on a steamboat. There we arrived all right.

When we arrived father fixed me up with money and clothing and left me with a family by the name of Will Rily. He left enough money with Rily to buy me more clothes in case I needed them. Father also paid my tuition in advance as long as the school was to last, which would be out on the first day of July. This school was the high school of St. Louis. There were seven teachers. The president's, or principal's, name was Man.

I started some time in January. The school was well attended, there being many scholars. I was well satisfied with the school and my boarding place. There was a boy there by the name of Tom Rily, who was Mr. Rily's son. Me and him liked one another as well as me and Jim. School got along fine and we learned very fast. I liked Tom and the boys and all the girls better than those in New York.

Everything went along nicely until about the last of February. That day the principal came very near whipping me. Torn Rily came very near having a whipping or a fight with a boy by the name of Johnson. One of the teachers put a stop to the trouble, and the boy's sister came up and began to raise Cain. I told her that a girl's place was among the girls. She said a lot of sassy things to me and I told her to go to thunder. The teacher sent me to the president to get a whipping. So I went up to take my medicine, and I told him what I had done. He made a long talk and told me the third time I came up he would have to whip me. I said there will never be a third time to you. School was surely fine and I learned fast. Mr. Rily wrote to father how fine I was getting along and what a good boy I was, and also how hard I studied.

About the middle of March Tom Rily received a whipping for whipping the Johnson boy. The only part I took in this was to look on and laugh. School was out about the first of July, and then we had a great time the Fourth of July. We surely had a fine time – a fine dinner and then a show that night. We enjoyed ourselves during the holidays.

School commenced again in October, when me and Tom started again. During the second week Tom came very near getting a whipping. Tom said to me that the freckle-faced girl did not know her spelling lesson very well. I said no. Her brother said, "Tom Rily, you are a liar, you scoundrel, and a red-headed one, at that." He had no more said the words when Tom hit him in the face with a water bucket, which came very near knocking him down. Both of us were on our way after water. Tom had no more than hit the boy with the bucket when one of the teachers seized him and beat him with his fist and dragged him around considerably. When he finished giving Tom a beating he told us to go on after our water, which we were glad to do. Tom was a little bit disfigured, as some hide was taken off his face. Tom said he felt a little bit funny, as though he had been shaken up.

School went along nicely the rest of the month of October. Mr. Rily was proud of the way me and Tom were learning, and wrote to father the way me and Tom were getting along. He also told father he believed it was the very thing for us two to be together. Father wrote he was very proud to hear such news, and said he was in hopes I would make a good man, and not continue being so mean as I had been in the schools before.

December came and then Xmas. Me and Tom had a hog-killing time. Mr. Rily had an eggnog and a fine dinner and lots of whiskey and wine. Me and Tom got to drinking too much and became drunk, when we commenced fighting, and Mr. Rily came out with a red strop, used for a razor hone. It was the heaviest I had ever seen used for that. He gave us a good whipping. The first thing he did was to throw me down and then Tom on top of me. And then he came very near beating Tom to death and then he put me on top and beat me accordingly. He then put Tom back and beat him some more and then says to me, "You are next again." He says, "You two are like a couple of hogs and don't know when you get enough." We finally got down and they put us to bed. We went to bed and got up next morning feeling bad. We were all right when New Year's came, but never got drunk any more.

School went along all right the rest of the year. Had another fine time Fourth of July. Father came up from the ranch and stayed during the time. Mr. Rily told father how much me and Tom were learning, and also told him we were thicker than thieves. Father told him he was going to keep me in school as long as he possibly could.

Chapter 9

ANOTHER TRIP TO GALVESTON AND THEN TO THE RANCH.

Father went back to the ranch about the twelfth of July and also took me with him. We boarded a steamboat for New Orleans. It was a pretty sight on the river. After we got to New Orleans we went on a ship to Galveston. After staying there a few days the boys came in from the ranch. Everything was getting along nicely. One of the boys got in a quarrel, which ended in shooting, with a Mexican over a game of cards. How it happened was thus: The greaser came and stayed all night, and while all except Henry Simpson were out looking after the horses and cattle, the Mexican proposed a game of cards. Simpson beat him and the Mexican got mad and attempted to kill Simpson with a knife, but five shots from Simpson's revolver sent him to his long home. This made father mad, and when we got to the ranch he told Simpson he could hunt another place, for he did not need him any longer, as it was against his orders for any one on the ranch to gamble. So in a day or so he left.

I began to ride my ponies and to enjoy myself with the cowmen. I got a letter from Jim Williams, wanting me to come and see him, but I thought I was through with that country – at least I thought so. In fact I was afraid to go back – afraid that those people might kill me. I wrote that I could not come.

I stayed around the ranch until about the first day of July. One day a small bunch of buffaloes came close to the ranch and a couple of the boys saddled their horses and mine and we gave chase. Every now and then they would shoot one down. I emptied the revolver they gave me. I don't suppose it hit anything. We rode back and told them we had four down. So the wagon was sent out, and they skinned a couple and furnished us with fresh buffalo meat as well as beef. The ones they skinned were very fine and the meat was excellent.

I began to think after this hunt I was ready to be an Indian fighter. I asked father if I could go out again with the boys. He said, "No, the Indians might get mad at us for killing his cattle, and then might want my scalp."

On the tenth or sometime in August we started to go on a fishing expedition, but seeing a large band of Indians, who were on their way to a Mexican settlement, we did not go any farther, thinking it best and safest for us if we did not do so as we did not want a fight with the boys.

During the month of August father and a few of his men went to Fort Brown after some horses he had bought from a Mexican, who lived close to Matamoros. Father let me go along also. We stayed at Fort Brown about seven days, and then went back to the ranch, arriving there the last days of August.

After staying there several days father made preparations to go to St. Louis, where I was to start school. Tom Rily wrote how much fun he was having, and I was ready to go. We went with a government outfit to Galveston, and after staying there several days and having a nice time, we boarded a mail ship for New Orleans.

After spending a few days there and seeing hardly anything but African negroes I became wearied, and begged father to go on to St. Louis. But father told me to be in no hurry and said he would go soon. At last we got on a steamboat for St. Louis, arriving there sometime in October. After we put up at a hotel for a day or so, we went to Mr. Rily's. During the days we were stopping at the hotel I ran into Tom. It was like a camp meeting when we got together. I went on home with Tom.

The first thing Mr. Rily asked was where father was. I told him he was around town somewhere, and I told him what hotel we were stopping at. He then picked up his hat and said, "The old skunk, I will collar him for not coming on here at first." Me and Tom went downtown to see our old friends. They were very glad to see me and I them, and when me and Tom did get back pa and Mr. Rily had their feet propped above their heads and talking. But me and Tom paid very little attention to them. We cared very little about associating with them and they with us, I suppose.

Father went back to New Orleans, and me and Tom went to school. We still had our fine time. About the twentieth of October me and Tom got a whipping for not learning a speech. I was not expecting a whipping the next time I went to the teacher, but I got it just the same. The worst of it was we had to learn the speech after all, and recite it, so we never gained anything by being so stubborn as a mule. Everything went along nice and we learned fast.

Mr. Rily wrote to father that me and Tom were doing better than was expected. And me and Tom fell in love with a couple of black-haired girls who were chums. So was me and Tom. They lived close together and were cousins. On Sunday, after dinner, me and Tom would always go to see them, and generally play some games, or went walking. So by constant attention we were deep in love. Christmas came and we went with them to the Christmas tree, and also to Mr. Rily's for dinner. Then we took them out walking and then back home. The teacher saw us and this was against the rules of his school. When January came he made a talk that some boys and girls had been seen going together, and said they should not do it, and if they did take the girls to amusements he would punish them for it. He said, "I mean this for a couple of boys and girls who are great friends." And said, "You had better mind and be very careful."

Me and Tom went walking after recess and had a talk over the subject, about which I will tell very little. Tom says, "That talk the old scoundrel made – isn't that a jaw breaker?" Tom says, "We will go to see them and he will never be any the wiser. And we will manage it so that he never will find it out. If we can get a talk with those girls we will arrange everything. So we made our talk to them, and they said they would tell nothing. We told them when we would be with them. So when Sunday came we went to the same Sunday school that they did. We were there quite a while before it commenced, and had a fine talk. The next Sunday was the same way. But the next Monday he had us boys and girls staying in school all day for trying to court and the coming evening he told us if this happened again he would whip us, and we took him at his word.

This was our last trip to see one another while school was going on. But after school was out we went to see them, until it began again. School was out in June. We had a fine time, if there was ever one. I began to think I could not get along without this girl. Father wrote and asked me if I wanted to come to the ranch and I said no, so he never came after me. School began again in September, with a new president, whose name was De Belevue, a Frenchman. He was an old man who had a fine education, and believed in boys and girls talking to one another. So me and Tom had a larpin time. We were at home only while school was not going on. Me and Tom were having such a fine time I was in hopes father would not take me home for a year or so. But you will see later.

October came and we had a nice time going to see our girls. I never learned as much as when that man was president, for it was study instead of play, or courting. Father heard me and Tom were courting so knew we were not learning, and said he was in hopes I would marry and move to the ranch. This made me smile. All I could think about was that girl.

It was not long before I was in a different frame of mind. Me and Tom went to a party and toward the last I asked her to be my partner. She said she would not, and I went and got another girl. She got up and played with another boy. I would not look at her any more. I told Tom what she had done. She would not tell the truth if she had to. It made me mad her acting that way, and then playing with that Roman-nosed boy. I was mad as Cain, in fact I had blood in my eye. We took them home and I never went back again. Tom's girl wanted me to come back again, but I said, "No." The other sent a lot of talk to me, but it was too late. She said she was not thinking of what she was doing. I told her it might bring her thinking qualities back to her, and she might take that other boy and eat him. They said she was in trouble. I considered our courtship was ended. And after this I learned a great deal more. I presume it was the best.

School went along nicely the rest of the year. January came and I was ready to go. I wrote to father when school was out to come after me, and he said he would. School went along nicely the rest of the year. I learned a great deal more than I had the months before. My girl wrote me a letter telling me she wanted me to come and see her, and said I was to come the next Friday night. She said she was sorry she had treated me so poorly. She said she loved me better than any boy she had ever seen before. She wrote, "Will you and Tom both come Friday night? I will also have my cousin come." I wrote and told her we would surely be there. So when I told Tom he was in great glee because I was going to see her again. When the night came I would not go, and the coming Monday laughed at her until she cried. It was the last time I ever wrote to her.

June came and father came up from the ranch and I went back with him. First to New Orleans, then to Galveston, and from there to the ranch. We got to the ranch about the second day of July. About the eighth day we began to gather a herd to take north. Father sold about five thousand steers to a man by the name of Yates, who lived up towards the head of the Colorado river. By the twentieth we were ready to start northward.

Chapter 10

FIRST YEAR A COWBOY. A BIG FIGHT WITH THE KICKAPOO INDIANS.

On the twenty-first we started north, well prepared to fight Indians, and had plenty of provisions
with us. I was proud to be a cowboy. Everything
went along nicely until the twenty-eighth. It being
rainy the cattle drifted badly and caused lots of
trouble. I was on guard with three men. The cows
drifted so badly we could not find the wagon again.
We had to arouse the other guards, so they could
relieve us. We had to stay until sunup, then they
came and relieved us. The wagon was moved but a
short distance, and we who had been up all night
lay down and slept on the grass until dinner. The
other boys gathered them up all right. About
August the second a thunderstorm came up and
scared our horses. It was pretty hard to find them
as they were scattered among the buffalo every-
where. We managed to find them all.

About the tenth or twelfth our men and father
had a fight with some Comanche Indians. There
were about twenty of the Indians in their crowd.

They were going to a Mexican settlement on the Rio Grande for ammunition. Seeing us on their left, they, having on their war paint, thought they would have some fun, so they came towards the men. After the revolvers and rifles of our men belched forth lead and fire, about one-half of their number were killed. They beat a retreat. We moved on northward and located camp for the night. One Indian came creeping around while one of the boys was watching the horses. He fired three shots and the Indian went away in a hurry. Nothing happened the rest of the night.

Next night we moved on the Frío creek, and the next we moved on the open plain. The cattle became frightened and ran terribly, but the boys managed to hold them in. The trouble with the cattle did not awaken me.

About the twentieth we moved on the Concho, where it empties into the Colorado. There we came on some Cheyenne Indians hunting. There were about five hundred in this gang – squaws, bucks, and children. They were peaceable. The next day some of us went fishing on the Colorado, or on the Concho, I meant to say, and caught a lot of fish, after which we had a fish fry at the camp wagon.

We stayed on the Concho three or four days, and then moved on a small creek called the Kickapoo, named after a tribe of Indians. We stayed on this creek several days, until the Kickapoo Indians scared our horses one night and stole part of them. While we were hunting them we came across a man by the name of Plaster. They had run his horses the same way as they did ours. So Plaster came on to our camp and told father that one of his men with some Texas Rangers had seen the horses in the possession of the Kickapoo Indians.

Plaster proposed to give them battle the coming night, and take the horses. So father had me and eleven more men fix up the firearms, leaving the other boys with the cattle and horses. We rode over to Plaster's camp and the Rangers rode up also. Plaster had thirteen of his men go, and that made ninety-six in all. So we rode out and sent two men ahead to locate the horses. They came back and told us there were two men with the horses, and over three hundred Indians camping in a thicket. One of our men, one of Plaster's, and a Ranger were sent to kill the Indians with the horses, which they did. As soon as they had done this we charged their camp and killed ten the first fire. We shot a great many afterwards.

We still stayed in the thicket with them until they made it so hot for us we had to get out. Pat Stevens got wounded and was left behind. We loaded our revolvers and said we would go back and get him. When we went in the Indian camp we discovered they had not noticed him, thinking we had gone. We charged back and run them out of most of the woods. We then carried away Stevens. We thought it best to leave them for they had so many more men than we. We all went back to Plaster's camp and divided our horses by moonlight. The Indians' horses were given to the Texas Rangers.

About the last of the month we moved up the Colorado river, and in the neighborhood of the fifteenth reached Yates' ranch. We only lost about three hundred cattle. Yates was a fine fellow, and said his ranch was a disagreeable one, that three of his men had been killed by Comanche Indians. He said he would move soon if troubles did not cease. It seemed as if they got worse instead of better.

On the eighteenth of September we headed for the ranch. We started south and had a fight with some Comanche Indians. We killed four horses and twelve Indians. We never had any more trouble the rest of the way, reaching the ranch about the fifteenth of October.

Father wanted me to go back to St. Louis again to school. I begged hard and told him I wanted a rest this year, and that I wanted to be with him at the ranch. He told me he was not going to be at the ranch, for he expected to spend the winter at Corpus Christi. He said he would let me know later whether he would send me to St. Louis or not. The only reason I did not want to go to St. Louis was on account of that love affair during the winter.

Chapter 11

FATHER AND I SPEND THE WINTER AT CORPUS CHRISTI. I FALL IN LOVE WITH A MEXICAN GIRL.

First of November came, and father never had said a word about St. Louis, and I was happy of it. On the second day of November father told me to get my rattletraps of clothing together, for he was going to Corpus Christi. Day of the fifth we started and reached the town the fifteenth of November. Arriving, we stopped at the Arney House, and stayed the rest of the year.

Mrs. Arney and her husband were part Spanish and English. They had a niece who was part English, Spanish, and Mexican. She was about sixteen, and me and father had been there but a short while before me and this girl were smiling. This happened every time we did meet. It was not long before we were courting. Father was downtown most of the time, but he soon noticed our actions toward one another, and most of the other people did also. Father said it beat a Dutch Jew the way I courted girls, and also said: "Son, if you ever get one you will have to court them, and when they are as pretty as this one, pin back your ears and fly at them." He reached for his paper and went to reading.

Christmas came and I was with my girl all the time. Father only looked at us, and laughed. Me and her got to waiting and eating together. I began to think that I could not get along without being where she was. She taught me the Spanish and Mexican languages.

We left Corpus Christi the second day. It took me and my loved one a long time before we could decide to separate. We arrived at the ranch about the tenth and everything was all right. The boys had been fighting among one another, but one good thing there were no firearms used.

About the twelfth father and his men began to gather a herd. He wished to gather his horses also. He sold the steers to a man by the name of Tom Hicks, who had a ranch about twelve miles southeast of Pecos City. The three thousand steers were gathered and we were ready to go up the trail. By the eighteenth we started up the Rio Grande. We stayed out far enough so the Mexican cow thieves would not annoy us. We reached Hicks' ranch about the last days of May.

We came back to the ranch about the fifteenth of June. Father and I stayed at the ranch several days. I got a letter from my girl at Corpus Christi, saying she wanted me to come back and see her. I asked father when he was going to Corpus Christi again. He said it would be a long time, and said he, "You can prepare yourself for St. Louis." This hurt me pretty bad, but it did no good. Father said he was not ready for me to marry a Mexican and might never be. Then I left the ranch and worked with the cow outfit until fall.

In September I got a letter from Tom Rily wanting me to come up and go to school. I did not want to go, but father told me to get my clothes ready, and said we would go to Galveston instead of Corpus Christi. We arrived in Galveston and then New Orleans. Then we boarded a steamer for St. Louis. We went to Mr. Rily's, and what a glad meeting it was for me and Tom.

We went to school and saw our old friends, and had a great time. Tom said our old girls went to a new country. I said glory go with them. Tom told me of a couple of boys of my age and his who had been trying to whip him, and he had stood them off. I told Tom the first time we came across them we would rear up with them. School went along nicely, and me and Tom enjoyed ourselves as well as the year before. We had no trouble with any of the boys. School was out in April, 1859. Father sent one of the men to come back with me so there would be no danger. I hated to leave Tom, but it was time for me to go.

On arriving at the ranch in July, there were several letters from Jim Williams of New York. He was wanting me to come and see him. I told father and he said I could go the first day of September.

About the first of August I went with some old worn-out Spanish cow ponies. Father had sold them to a man who lived at Corpus Christi. Arriving at Corpus Christi and having delivered our horses, I went to see Mrs. Arney. She told me my girl had married a rich Mexican, who lived in Old Mexico, about six months before. This did not grieve me very much as I had been away so long. We started back to the ranch and got back about the twentieth.

By the fifth day of September I was in New York at Mrs. Williams' place. They were very proud to see me, and I them. And they told me all the news, and said there was no danger for me to stay there now, as the boy I had shot had left the country. Mrs. Williams asked about father. I told her he wanted an excuse to come up to see her. Christmas came and me and Jim had a fine time going to dances and parties, and had a great time.

Everything went nicely the rest of the year of 1859 and 1860, with the exception of the election of the President, for people were anxious to see who would succeed Buchanan. The people were divided into four parties, but the Republicans carried the day, on account of several things – the slave law and so forth. Five states had withdrawn from the Union. Still a great many men of the Northern states wished something to be done to bring back the states that had withdrawn. Some things were done but nothing was accomplished for the states, and people thought they had been imposed upon. The slave law was wrong on their part, and the Southerners, having their minds set, were determined on secession.

Chapter 12

THE WAR OF SECESSION AND THE FIRST BATTLE AT BULL RUN – WE ARE BADLY DEFEATED IN THIS BATTLE.

I will write now about the Civil War in the United States. This war started with the firing on Fort Sumter, in 1861, and ended at the surrender of the Confederate armies in 1865. It lasted four years. This was the worst war described in history. The struggle was waged with enormous armies, upon a great and vast territory. It was a terrible destruction to life, and was the most grievous that ever had occurred. It involved the people who had been the most happy and prosperous on the face of the earth.

Abraham Lincoln was inaugurated President of the United States March 4, 1861. Hamline, of Maine, was chosen vice-president. Lincoln, in his address, declared it was not lawful for any state to withdraw from the Union, and furthermore said his intention was not to interfere with the slavery of the South, but was to protect the property of the United States. It was his duty to see that the arsenals, which the seceders had seized, were restored, and the forts abandoned at once.

The Southern army began to organize after their congress met at Montgomery. Their army numbered close to four thousand. Some of the troops were placed under Beauregard, who bombarded the captured Fort Sumter April 12, 1861.

After the fall of Fort Sumter President Lincoln called for seventy-five thousand volunteers, who came forward in great numbers. In a very short while there was a large force around Washington, which was placed under Scott. General Winfield Scott was placed commander-in-chief.

My father was well acquainted with Scott and I received permission to go with the scouts. Our army remained close, watching the Confederates. In June we commenced to make a forward movement, very slowly. The Confederates, under Beauregard, still lay at Manassas Junction.

Our army was called the "Army of the Potomac" and the Southern army, the "Army of Northern Virginia." Richmond was the capital of the Southern Confederacy. It became the Northern troops' cry, "On to Richmond." General Scott became excited and ordered a forward movement, which was done July the sixteenth. McDowell was in advance and we scouts were ahead of him. After the scouts and others had a great deal of skirmishing, at the Fort and Centerville early one Sunday morning, our army reached Bull Run. Behind the army of Beauregard was posted.

Our soldiers commenced the battle, which lasted the greater part of the day, and was fought with great determination on both sides. Our troops drove the Confederate wings almost off the battle-field, and would have taken the whole field if the Confederates under General Jackson had not cut our army in two pieces and forced the remainder to flee to Washington. The roads were crowded with soldiers in retreat. We scouts could keep out of the way, as we were well mounted.

After the Battle of Bull Run, Lincoln knew that a terrible war was at hand, and called for over a half-million of troops, which were placed under General George McClellan. His army numbered over 160,000. The Confederates also received large reinforcements, and still camped at Manassas Junction. Nothing of importance happened the rest of the year, except that a United States warship stopped a British ship and captured two Confederates who acted as commissioners. Old England came very near fainting and we would have had to give her another whipping if we had not given them up. As they were of no benefit to us and too much trouble to feed, we gave the men up.

Chapter 13

CAMPAIGN IN 1862.

General U.S. Grant made a naval and land campaign, and captured forts right and left. This put the Confederates in great danger and shook their center. The Confederates after this, in order to check Grant, decided to give battle. Albert Sidney Johnston gave Grant battle at Shiloh and drove his army to the shelter of the gunboats. Grant received reinforcements and the Confederates retreated in return.

Our scouts were ordered to go to Rosecrans' army at Nashville. Near the last of December the Confederates attacked our army and drove us from the field. The battle lasted all day.

The Battle of Murfreesboro, or Stone River, called by some, began December 31 and lasted five days. The Confederates began the battle and drove us off the field. As fast as one would take the field the other would retake it. This continued all day, for the two armies fought with determination.

January came and with it another fearful battle, which gave no gain to either. It was a fearful day.

Day of the second was as the former. It was a sickening sight to see the dying and wounded, and it was a lamentable one also.

The day of the third came and our General was informed by us scouts that the noted cavalry man, Wheeler, was on his way to attack our wagon train, which was loaded with provisions. He ordered us scouts and some more to go to the aid of the wagons and help resist the Confederates. Wheeler came and when he saw the wagons surrounded by us bluecoats he was surprised and stopped to gaze a few moments. But as he was anxious to burn our wagons, they charged on us. They came like the birds, they came so fast. We brought them to a dead stand and then repulsed them. They then retreated, leaving many dead men and horses behind, while many horses went back riderless. The battle was soon ended, which was a defeat to the Confederates, who were forced to leave the city.

During the year of 1862 several naval battles occurred. The most remarkable one was the fight between the Merrimac and Monitor, in Hampton Roads. The Merrimac was an ironclad constructed by the Confederates at Norfolk. On the eighth day of March she came out on the Union fleet and after a battle destroyed the sloop-of-war Congress. This ship was built and plated with railroad iron. Cannon bails would have had no more effect on it than pitching gravels on a floor. This Confederate ironclad returned again and destroyed the ship Cumberland. It seemed as though nothing could stop it from destroying our fleet.

It came again to destroy the Minnesota, but a new warship was on hand and saved the Minnesota. Its name was the Monitor. The Merrimac had taken off some of her iron rigging. The Monitor was an ironclad vessel also and was built at New York.

The Minnesota was set on fire two or three times. After hours of fighting the Merrimac steamed off to Norfolk and at the same time the Monitor went to shallow water. The Merrimac made a mistake when she took off some of her rigging, for the Monitor battered her up considerably. The Monitor had gotten a hole through her, but was the means of saving the fleet. The Merrimac came to Hampton Roads two or three times but there were no more battles.

When the Union troops captured the Confederate navy yard the Confederates tried to get the Merrimac to Richmond during a high tide, or while the stream was up, but were unable on account of it being so heavy. Then the Confederates destroyed her.

After the Battle of Murfreesboro a great many of us scouts were ordered to the Army of the Potomac, which was under Burnside. About the last days of January he was relieved of the command, which was given to Hooker. General Hooker moved to attack Lee, who was still at Fredericksburg.

Hooker said he was not going to have a big battle at Fredericksburg the way Burnside had. We moved above Fredericksburg so Lee would be compelled to fight us in the open field. After our army had moved about twenty miles above Fredericksburg Lee was forced to take a great part of his army and come to meet us. This resulted in the great Battle of Chancellorsville.

Stonewall Jackson rushed out on the flank and this part had their arms stacked. It was so unexpected that they made us flee from camp and Jackson placed the Confederate flag within a mile of Hooker's camp. If night had not come on, our entire army would have been destroyed.

The heaviest battles were fought on the second day of May. This was a great loss and we were forced to retreat on May 5. This grieved Lincoln and caused dissatisfaction in the North, for our force was more than two to one.

President Lincoln was not satisfied with his generals. It seemed that Grant was the only one who had made success all the way through. Our army had been defeated at Bull Run and Chancellorsville, and the only great battle we had gained was at Murfreesboro.

Lee had invaded Pennsylvania, and resolved to attack the North the second time, having received large reinforcements, which made his army number about seventy thousand. He now moved northward, the reason was that he wished to carry on the war in Northern territory.

Hooker was relieved of command by Meade, and we had to fall back to defend Washington. The armies met at Gettysburg, where a battle was fought the first and third days of July. The Confederates were badly defeated in this battle.

After this they moved up and placed themselves on the south side of the Rapidan and the Northern army moved up and took position on the north. They were stationed here the remainder of the year of 1863. No trouble occurred in the meantime. Operations in the West and Southwest were favorable to the Union.

Chapter 14

THE LAST DAYS OF THE CONFEDERACY – CAMPAIGN OF 1864 AND 1865 ENDS THE WAR.

General U.S. Grant was made commander of all the armies. Lee was still guarding the line of the Rapidan, but our army crossed the river and engaged the Confederates in the bloody Battle of the Wilderness, with fearful loss of life. This battle lasted three days.

Grant resolved to get between Lee and Richmond by a flank movement, but Lee was faster and placed his army behind earthworks. Our army tried for three weeks to carry this plan through but only one man and his command succeeded and captured three thousand men. Giving up this Grant tried another flank movement, to see if he could get between Lee and Richmond, but Lee moved faster and placed his army in front of us at the North Ana.

In repeating this movement it brought the Army of the Potomac up to the Chickahominy, where it met a disastrous defeat. We met a disastrous defeat at Cold Harbor. Grant soon saw that he could not approach Richmond from that route. So he made a change and had his army cross the James river. After Grant had done this Lee fell back in the earthworks of Richmond and Petersburg. The battles of the Rapidan and the James cost thousands of lives.

Our hopes in crossing the James river was to capture Petersburg before it could be fortified. Our army made an assault but failed, and a great many other attempts also failed. Grant said there would have to be a siege, and it would take some time to wear them out. A tunnel was dug under Petersburg, and after having done that we were to capture it. The Confederates heard us digging under the earth, and when it was blown in the air our troops rushed forward to capture the city, but the Confederates were prepared and forced our soldiers to retreat from the great volley of shot and shell. So this failed.

I will now give an account of a vessel which destroyed so much of our commerce. Its name was the Alabama. It was at last sunk by one of our vessels off the coast of France in 1865.

Lee's troops still lay in their works around Richmond and Petersburg, but his situation was hopeless. He planned an attack on Fort Stedam, which he captured but was soon driven out. An assault on Richmond and Petersburg carried many points. Lee retreated, hoping to join Johnston, but was surrounded at Appomattox Court House. When Johnston heard of Lee's surrender he surrendered to Sherman. Lee's surrender caused the greatest joy through the North.

President Lincoln was shot in a theatre in Washington. Booth, after shooting the President, fled away in Maryland, but was overtaken and shot. Secretary Seward was also stabbed the same night that Lincoln was shot. There seemed to be a number of people in league with Booth and a great many were hanged.

At the death of President Lincoln, Andrew Johnson, who had served as vice-president, was made President. After the war was over and our army was disbanded I went back to St. Louis and worked for wages for a while.

Chapter 15

AFTER THE WAR WENT BACK TO THE LONE STAR STATE AND FOLLOWED THE WILD LIFE OF A COWBOY.

I stayed around St. Louis until a steamer went to New Orleans. I then boarded one, and in a few days I was off to Galveston on another boat. While staying there I met a man who was a near ranchman to father. This man said they had had a hard time during the war. He said they and father's men stayed on the Old Mexico side in order to keep from being in the war. He said they would come out once in a while to brand the calves so they would know them when they got older.

He said, "Come with me and we will go to your father's ranch. We got to Mr. Randal's ranch about the first of June. He said father, not hearing from me, supposed I was killed. We rode down to father's ranch about the sixth of June. He was glad to see me. The first thing he said was, "That fellow you have looks like a war horse."

The range was loaded with unbranded cattle. About the twelfth we went to branding. There were lots of them, part of the increase during the war. It was great counting all. We employed lots of Mexicans and branded until November. We had a great herd.

Father gave me a brand and when fall came I had over one thousand head. I spent most of my time with the boys branding, and when spring came I had a drove. Everything was branded by April, 1866.

Father made a trip to Matamoros, where he had spent part of the time during the war, and I went with him. We stayed there about a month watching the card playing and gambling. Father was pretty good and taught me.

We went back to the ranch and stayed awhile with the boys, and then put in our time at Fort Brown, now called Brownsville. I got to be a popular fellow around Fort Brown. I was well prepared in the way of a good education, and the soldiers all liked me. I was elected squire.

One of the lieutenants wanted to get married to a captain's girl and I was called to marry them the coming night. I said to father I didn't know how to marry anyone. He only laughed, and said, "You will have to take your medicine; say something, for they want to marry." I was somewhat confused never having seen but one or two married. Of course this does not help one much unless they study or observe much. I knew it would never do to show weakness.

The night came and they came after me, so me and father went down. Father had a smile on his face like the wave on a small lake, thinking of the trouble I was in.

The house was crowded. I went up to the front where the couple were and everything was ready. I told the couple they would please rise. The first thing I did was to have a chair put in front of them and the Holy Bible placed on it open, and I said to the man, "Are you willing to swear that you will protect this woman, and love her and always treat her right?" He said he was. I asked the girl if she would treat him right and show him respect. She said she would.

I told them they might kneel at the Bible and chair, and I said to the man, "If you ever fall short of this I am in hopes the tongue may be cut out of your mouth." I then said to the woman, "If you don't fulfill your oath I am in hopes your days will be unhappy."

To both I said, "This being the first time either of you were ever married I will require you to kiss the book only once. I now, by God who I worship, and the Holy Saint John, pronounce you man and wife. The friends, while you stand, may shake your hands and wish you happiness."

The crowd roared with laughter. I now took my seat with the others, and a great many said they had to shake hands with me. I told them it was my first couple and if anything was left out I was to blame for not looking it up, and if I had known it I might have told something else. My father and some others laughed a week. If I knew there was another couple to marry I think I would have skipped.

We stayed around Fort Brown until about the tenth of July. Then we went to the ranch and stayed until branding was over.

In the fall, about November, he and father went back to Fort Brown and stayed the winter. A Scotchman from Scotland, who had a ranch near Pecos City, wanted to buy some cattle and father sold him ten thousand head. We were to deliver them in the spring.

Spring came and we began to gather our herd, and by the last of May we were ready to start up the Rio Grande and the Rio Pecos. Father went ahead with the first herd of about four thousand. The next herd was under Arthur Gray, and the last was under my management.

In about four days we came above the salado, where a creek empties in the Rio Grande. My herd caused lots of trouble and ran a great deal on our guard but me and three others managed to keep them from getting away. I went out as soon as they began to cause trouble. The buffalo were a nuisance, for they would mix with our cattle during the night. We would run them out when the morning came. The boys shot some of the buffalo just for sport. The few cattle that had gotten away were gathered the next morning. We then followed on after the other herds.

In July we had a hard drive to get to the Junta creek, which took two days and nights. When our advance cattle began to get to the water the others were twelve miles behind. It being so dry and they walking so fast they were in by 1:30. The dust was flying a mile high. We let them drink lots of water and then moved about a mile and camped for the night.

We had a nice trip from there on, with plenty of grass and water. We delivered the cattle about the twelfth of August, and got back to the ranch about the fifteenth of September. Wheeler had branded all the calves during our absence. All me and father did was to sit around.

We stayed at Fort Brown from October until January 1, 1868. During the winter the Indians came down and invaded our neighborhood, and when a settler would go out to locate in their wagons, which were covered with sheets, the Indians would circle around them and kill their horses and then murder the men, women, and children. When the soldiers would come the Indians would keep out of their way. They did not know what to do with the Indians. I said, "If you will let me have a lot of soldiers I will fix the red scoundrels. I will have them so they will wish they had never seen a covered wagon or immigrant train."

The commander asked when I would want the soldiers and I said in three days. I had the scouts locate the large Indian camp. They said it was about forty miles above, and guessed there must be over a thousand camped. I will tell you later about this drive by their camp.

After three days everything was nearly ready. We arranged seats and the men were to come out when the proper time came. On the fourth day our wagons, ten in number, and covered with sheets, were ready. We had about two hundred men, four cooks, and provision wagons that we had hidden.

We drilled at the fort, and learned every place a man was to take when the battle was on. How he was to jump out and act when the right time came. The cooks and drivers were to watch the teams and horses.

The fourth day came and we drove within twenty-six miles of the Indian camp. Some Indians began to watch us, and one black scoundrel tried to get a shot at me; but the very instant he came in view I put a bullet hole through him with my Springfield rifle.

We camped before sundown with the Indians still watching us. I suppose they were the lookouts. I ordered all but fifteen men to stay in the wagons. We cooked supper and when it began to get sundown the Indians went away.

At night we placed a heavy guard, and by sunup we were all ready to go in the wagons but five, who were on horseback. There were some Indians watching us, and when we drove to the right of the Indian camp, about twelve men began to surround us. The Indians came from the hills in vast numbers. I ordered the wagons stopped in order to make preparations for the fight. There were about eight hundred Indians, but appeared to be three thousand. I told the men to go to work. The bullets were screaming past us. The Indians began to circle around us, and when our men began to use their firearms and revolvers for a while there were about 360 Indians down, and the ground covered with horses. They soon saw their mistake and beat a retreat. I ordered the men to kill the wounded Indians, for the commander had said we should leave none. One Indian shot a fellow, and the boys butchered them right and left.

After the boys had relieved the dead Indians of their firearms, we drove back to the Fort. We lost in this Indian fight only twelve men. We got back to the Fort all right and gave the news. The people were very proud of our luck in killing so many of the red lads. From this time on I never knew of an Indian attacking a covered wagon. I don't know whether this taught them a lesson or not, but can say it was the last time they disturbed our part of the country.

We stayed around Fort Brown quite a while and then went back to the ranch. Me and three others went on a buffalo hunt, for they began to drift in our range in large bunches. An Englishman came in and wanted some hides, so we employed about ten Mexicans to skin them and we went to killing. In about four days we had the number he wanted and he gave us two dollars apiece and therefore we made a great deal of money. It had taken lots of them off our cattle range.

Chapter 16

I MAKE ANOTHER TRIP TO FORT BROWN. SHOOTING SCRAPE WITH TWO MEXICANS AND A NEGRO.

About the tenth of June, me and Charlie Byars went on a pleasure trip to Fort Brown. After staying there a day or so Byars had to hunt a place to gamble, and he found it, too. He lost all his money and came back and told of his bad luck. I let him have some more money.

He then went off to a gambling house run by two Mexicans and a negro. I followed up and sauntered in as if I knew no one. The game went on until about ten, and Byars' luck was pretty good. The negro got behind him and began to make signs. I said to Byars, "That negro is telling what you have." Byars said, "He never will tell again," and drawing his revolver shot him twice, and the Mexicans made for him with knives, but they bit the dust just the same. The gambling table was relieved of its money and me and Byars went out a back way and they never did find out who killed them.

We stayed around a few days to keep down suspicion, then we rode out to the ranch and branded calves all summer, and late that fall me and father made another trip to Fort Brown. I did not stay very long, but came back and put in the time branding, hunting and killing buffalo.

Next spring I drove a herd of cattle to Corpus Christi, and when I returned me and Wheeler drove two more herds for father to a place where San Angelo now stands. We made this drive about June. We arrived and delivered our herd the twenty-fifth of August, and on the twenty-eighth we were on our way back.

On our second day's journey me and two others went on a hunting expedition. We were a long way from the other boys, when all at once a bunch of Cheyenne and Comanche Indians came on us. After surrounding us they tried to kill us, but we got out and ran away. I told the boys we would have to separate, which we did, and the other boys shot three or four apiece and got away from the ones pursuing them. When they got close to me I would kill two or three in rapid succession with my revolvers. One tried three times to lance me but I am satisfied I shot him four or five times before he fell. The other boys were close by this time and the Indians went their way and left me.

We got back to the ranch about the fifteenth of September. Stayed around there quite a while and then me and father went on a visit to Matamoros, where we spent the winter months. Nothing of importance happened, only Byars came in from the ranch to drink and gamble. After staying there quite a while he was killed by a Mexican by the name of Jean Mortina, who was a murderer and horse and cattle thief, and who stole his cattle and horses from Texans. Me and father went down to see the cause of his death and we found they had murdered him in cold blood. I swore if the chance ever came I would kill the ones that did this.

We stayed at Matamoros all winter. I found out there were two in the gang which killed him in cold blood. We went back to the ranch in April. I did nothing but hunt.

The first of May, 1869, we took another herd of cattle to a creek above old Fort Chadborne. It was an old fort. We had a great deal of trouble with our cattle, but delivered them in August. This country was loaded with buffalo and Indians, and the Cheyennes gave me a chase one day, but I, having a better horse, outran them. Sometimes you would see an arrow in a buffalo. We got back to the ranch in September and found a lot of Mexicans hunting horses during this month. The Mexicans were under a fellow by the name of Mortina. He was doing some hunting and one night he never came in, and the greasers made a search for him. They found him dead with five bullet holes through him. The Mexicans swore we had done this. We told them we were not going to be accused of anything unless we did it. We told them if they did not leave we would kill the whole bunch, so they went on their way rejoicing.

During the winter I put in most of my time hunting and branding wild cattle. Along in March I went on a trip to Fort Brown, and was told by one of the officers that one of the Mexicans, whose brother had been killed that winter when me and Byars were there, had said I was the one who had done it, he believed. The officer told me to watch him or he might kill me. This Mexican began to make ugly glances at me. He was pointed out so I would know him. One night the Mexicans had a ball. I was there and so was this Mexican. He asked me if he could talk to me and I said no, for I wanted to talk to a certain girl, so he would have to excuse me. Stepping aside he drew a double-edge knife and came toward me. As rapidly as thought I shot him six times. The officers arrested me, but turned me loose. I never was tried before any court. After the shooting I left for the ranch.

In June, July, and August I helped brand cattle, but never went up the trail with any herd. There was only one herd taken up, and Wheeler and the men did this.

During that fall I went to St. Louis to see my old home, where I used to board and go to school. Tom Rily was out in the country farming. I went out to see him. He told me his father and mother were rich and were living in Rhode Island. I stayed at Tom's home all winter, and what a time we had. Tom was in need of money, and I let him have a lot. April, 1871, came and I begged Tom to go back to the ranch with me and quit that farming. He said he would.

By the first of May he was ready to go. We boarded a steamer for New Orleans, and, staying there a few days, went on another to Galveston. From this city we went to the ranch, getting there about June. Father said he was glad to see us. He said to Tom he was glad to see my old friends with me, that I needed a friend, and it was for him to feel at home. Me and Tom enjoyed ourselves. Tom enjoyed hunting for he was not used to such a life.

One day four Indians, while we were hunting, thought they would try us a round, but we shot two horses out from under them and they let us alone. We prowled around and went on to the ranch, and told the boys about the Indians trying to kill us. The boys only laughed and told Tom they wanted his red scalp, that it was dangerous for red-headed people to get out on the cattle range, that is, if there were any Indians about. Tom said he would not have any business so far off any more.

Chapter 17

I TAKE A PARTNER IN THE CATTLE TRADE, AND FATHER'S OPINION. HE SAYS A WOMAN SHOULD BE THE ONE.

Next morning I asked father if he cared if I took Tom as a partner. He said he cared not, but that I had better take some girl, as they are the best partners. He then told us to get out of his sight, so me and Tom went and put some wild Spanish horses in the corral and rode them. It was not long before Tom was an expert and could ride any wild horse. By hunting and riding we became expert marksmen.

We put in the rest of the summer helping brand cattle, and spent most of the winter of 1871 at Matamoros. Me, father, Tom, and Thompson stayed at Matamoros during the winter. Thompson was a cousin to Byars who was killed at this place in the past. He wished to kill the other Mexican, who killed him or helped do it. I told him I would point him out so that he would know him when he came across him.

We were around the gambling dens and I pointed him out. He was running a gambling den in another part of the town. All we had to do was to eat and watch these places. We found out that late at night the owners were the only ones there. One night towards daylight these men were killed. Whan Dios was among them. When this was done everyone had gone to bed. No one paid any attention to it, thinking someone had gotten drunk and was having some fun. Who did the killing the author will not say.

We went around town, but were heavily armed, as all the people were in those days. We left for the ranch in April. On about May 3 we began to collect a herd of horses to take to a fellow who lived on the Colorado river. His name was Greely. Father sold this man about three thousand head of old steers. He had two ranches, one on the San Sabba, and the other on the Colorado, right in the angle of the river. About the eleventh, Wheeler started north with the herd and me and Tom went with him. We delivered the herd about the tenth of July and started back to the ranch. We did not have any trouble with the Indians this time. We got back to the ranch about the first day of August.

There was a boy who worked with me and Tom whose name was Jim James. He was a fine fellow, and during the fall he went to Fort Brown with a couple of mean fellows, whose nicknames were Jim Adair and Lone Jack. They murdered him in cold blood, and made their escape to southern Kansas and the Indian Territory. One of them went to work on the Cimarron river in the Indian Territory, and the other went south of Kiowa, Kansas. Lone Jack was on the Cimarron, and in a very short while me and Tom agreed to go to that country, and see if we could see him.

In the spring of seventy-two, me and Tom went to Galveston, and from there to St. Louis. There we loaded up our firearms and went to the Territory with a government outfit. We had a lonely trip up the Cimarron river. Tom went to Kiowa and I went to the Territory. Tom located his man and went to work on the same ranch. They became great friends. He told Tom about killing a young fellow at Fort Brown, and he should not have done it. About August 2 there was a man missing, and on searching they found him dead and scalped. It was Adair. Tom stayed there until the first day of September and then called for his money and horse and rode down on the Cimarron, which was in the Indian Territory.

Well, I will tell you how I came out, After me and Tom separated on the Cimarron, I went to work on the river. I worked until the thirtieth day of July, and during that time made two trips with herds of cattle to Caldwell, Kansas. But that day I got my money from the man who ran this wagon. The man Lone Jack was with the round-up. There was a fight at the round-up after the cattle were run in. There were revolvers used and after it was over one man said there were other revolvers used. Of course the excitement ran high. They did not know. There was only one man killed and his nickname was Lone Jack.

I stayed there until the fifth day of September. Tom came, and we made a lonesome trip down the Cimarron. The first day we did not have much to eat, for we were afraid to shoot the wild animals. The country looked as though it was full of Indians by the fresh signs. We killed a deer for dinner and roasted enough for supper, so we need not build a new fire.

Next day we came across a government outfit and went to St. Louis with them. We told them we were lost, and would like to go with them. They said all right. We arrived at St. Louis about the twenty-fifth of September. We took passage on a steamboat the fifth of October for New Orleans, staying there about ten days. We got on a kind of mail ship and went to Galveston and from there to the ranch.

Branding was all over and everything was moving along nicely. Me and Tom stayed all winter at the ranch, and put in the time roping long-eared yearlings.

During the spring and summer me and Tom went on a trip to New York city and stayed there all summer. We enjoyed ourselves very much. We found a couple of girls, and the way we paid attention to them was a caution. That fall we came back to the ranch. The first thing we did was to go to Matamoros, and we stayed there during the winter months. We paid attention to a couple of Mexican girls, and their people tried to stop us. We came very near killing a whole bunch of them, but they got us stopped just the same. It was no little trouble for them to do it. In the spring of seventy-five Frank and Jim Smith, two guerrillas who used to be with Quantrell during the war, became good friends to Tom and me. They liked us, is what I meant. We were together a great deal.

During the summer and late in the fall three and four gangs of Mexicans began to steal cattle on the Rio Grande and take them to Old Mexico. The Smith boys' ranch was about twenty miles above ours. Jim Smith proposed to kill those Mexicans and take the cattle and go in the ranch business on a large scale.

In a few days a Mexican and his men came with a bunch of two thousand cattle. They had stolen them from an Englishman who lived about a hundred miles away on the Rio Pecos. The reason they did not cause very much trouble was because so many soldiers were close by. If they would have tried it we would have ragged with them. A bunch of Mexicans came along about twenty miles above the Smith brothers' ranch. About seven of us went out and killed the ones with the horses, and then we rushed on the others and had a big fight, killed them all, and took the cattle. The first thing we did was to drive the horses back the way they had come from to keep down suspicion, finally turning them loose. All of these cattle were given to the Smith brothers, as they did not have many. Tom learned from one of the Mexicans that there was another herd behind, which would be in in about five days and they had about three thousand. So Tom blew out the Mexican's brains and went on.

We stayed around the Smith brothers' ranch until that other herd was getting pretty close. We came very near having a killing among our own men. The cause of the trouble was over the Civil War. Jim Young got to talking about how the Southern people had been imposed upon and then began to abuse the North. Red-headed Tom told him if it made no difference he had rather not hear such talk, and said, "I am in hopes you will stop." Young said, "You may want to stop me." "Yes," said Tom, "I will stop you," and reached for his revolver, but we put a stop to it. I got up and made a talk and told them they were a mean class on both sides, that they should have been burnt alive, and told them never to mention the war again. I asked Jim Smith what he thought about it. He said anyone was a fool to mention the past.

We got everything settled all right and began to get ready for that other herd of cattle. The first cattle did not want to stay in their new range. But the cowboys forced them by riding hard after them. It was getting time for that other herd to be close, from what the dying Mexican had said, so we began to get our firearms in working order, and had them in up-to-date trim before they came.

Chapter 18

ANOTHER CATTLE RAID AND ONE OF MR. PINK'S DETECTIVES COMES TO SEE US.

Me and Frank Smith rode about twenty miles up the river to locate the other herd. It was making for the same crossing as the other, but we were determined they should never reach it. We started back but did not get very far. We stopped at an irrigated farm owned by a German, and asked to stay all night. He asked us where we were going. We told him to Fort Brown. He asked us what we were doing in that part of the country. We told him looking after horses. He said there were a lot in that part of the country, which seemed to be going up the country. We told him we had seen a great many but they were not ours, as ours might have gone the other way. He told us about the Mexicans getting so mean and stealing Texas cattle and killing the cowboys. I said to Smith we had better be careful and go back, for they might run across us. He treated us mighty well, giving us a bed and feeding our horses. After paying him we went on our way, he telling us to come and see him again. We invited him to see us if he ever came to Fort Brown. Bidding him adieu, we rode down the Rio Grande to the ranch. We got in a little while before dark.

Next morning we rode out with a camping outfit, so we could work on them early. We camped about eight miles from the Mexican herd.

Next morning we went for them and in the fight killed all. Three tried to get away, but Jim Smith and Tom ran after and killed them. They came back and we had a talk whether we would keep the horses or not. We were in favor of keeping them, but Jim Smith said, "If we do they will locate the cattle and we had better put them on the other side of the river," which we did. We took the cattle to the ranch and let them scatter over the range.

Jim Smith said we had better leave a man to watch for that other herd, so we left Jim Amos to do the work. Amos said he was sick and would ride out in day time and stay at the German's at night. Jim said he would look for horses when the day would come. That's what he would claim. Well, after we got the cattle where there was plenty of water and range, we went on to the ranch.

Next day, after twelve, a fellow rode up and asked if he could work for us. One of the boys called me out and told me what he wanted. Not liking his looks I called out Frank Smith, and asked him if he wished to employ that man. Frank said yes, and at the same time covered him with his revolver, and said, "Get down," and Jim Smith came out. He was soon tied and relieved of his fire-arms. Frank said, "James, do you know him?" Jim said, "No." Frank said, "This is one of old Pink's men. I know him for we robbed him once before, and I came very near killing him."

I took a watch and fifty dollars. Frank said, "You are not satisfied in running us away from our homes, but follow us you will never again." He denied everything, but Frank said, "It is no use, you are at your journey's end." The man asked them to leave him free. "Yes," Frank said, "We will let you go, but it will be to a tree."

Frank asked what we should do with him. Jim said, "We have done lots of work on the river." After supper was over he was tied on a horse and taken on the river and swung up to a tree in a thick bunch of timber. How long he stayed I could not say, for the last time I was there he was still swing-ing.

The boys came in late and no one came after work. If they had I guess I would have given them work until they came in. Next day we shot some buffalo and shoved our new cattle down the river. They seemed to be anxious to get back to their old home, and we wished them to stay on the other side of the ranch, towards Fort Brown.

That night father came in and stayed with us. He told us he had sold all of his cattle but about four thousand, and said the man was going to move them right away. If me and Tom wished to go with him he would sell everything. No, we told him, we would stay on the Rio Grande. He said, "What cattle I leave, you and Tom can have." So the man came and father and we delivered them.

After the cattle were gone father left men to take care of mine and Tom's cattle. So we and the Smiths owned the range and prepared to stock it. Jim Amos came in and said another herd of cattle was coming and there were about five thousand head.

We went out and camped and next day we went at the cowboys and scattered and killed all of them. We had one man killed in this battle. We took him to a secret place and buried him, while the other boys were taking the cattle on. When we came from the funeral we burned the wagons and left the horses there. So we went our way and were soon at the ranch.

In a day or so there was a man I must speak of, a ranchman, who lived on the Old Mexico side. I was well acquainted with him for he kept coming to see me and Jim Smith. His name was Sid Sutton, who was a well-to-do cattleman, and had a Mexican for a wife. Us boys would go and see him every now and then. I will speak of this man again. We and the Smith boys went in full partnership.

We were soon to need some money, and did not want to sell any cattle to get it either, so Jim Smith proposed to go where they carried gold from Chihuahua, a city in Mexico, and capture a mule train load of it. Jim said, "Go and I will show you." Leaving our ranch in charge of good men, we went to a watering place east of Monclova, and stayed there a few days. I must tell how we were dressed. We had fine clothes and hats and boots, and looked like Sunday school teachers. Finally a mule train came along loaded with gold and silver.

Chapter 19

WE RELIEVE THE MEXICANS OF THEIR GOLD AND SILVER AND THEN TAKE A TRIP TO GALVESTON.

When the manager came along we asked him if we could go to the City of Mexico with them. He seemed to hesitate. We told him we were afraid to go by ourselves on account of Indians. We knew no Indians were in that part of the country. He said all right. First day they watched us closely. Next day was the same and the four or five days following.

Jim Smith gave the sign. The Mexicans seemed to think everything was all right. They had stacked their firearms. They had four men guarding them. All at once Smith gave a whistle and shot them dead. It took us no time to pack the mules for we had them to do it by saying we would kill them. After getting everything ready we bade them adieu. We told them we would kill any that would follow us. In this way we left them fifty miles from anywhere. They had to walk. We went between the two ranches.

The Smith brothers and us went in full partnership. We at last got to Galveston and sold the gold and silver for sixty thousand, and the mules for two thousand. After we made our sale we went on a steamer bound for New Orleans. We stayed around there about a month, having a fine time with the people. We got in a gambling den that let us come and play with them, and the way we enjoyed ourselves was a caution. We put in our time seeing the dens and gambling. We never drank. Me and Frank stayed at one place and Jim and Tom at another.

After staying there a month, we disguised ourselves and went back to Galveston and after staying there a while we went to Corpus Christi and thence to the ranch. As soon as we arrived at the ranch the cowboys told us of Sid Sutton's death, and also of Dave Morgan's, an old friend of mine. There were only three living on the ranch, his wife and two Mexicans, twelve having been murdered.

We rode over to make inquiries about this. Jim was so mad that he swore he would kill the one that murdered Sutton and before life was out of him would cut out his tongue and show it to him. I said to Jim, "I will help, but I think it is enough without a tongue, they being dead." I said, "You had better say you are sorry and not take such an oath as you may not get to fulfill it." Jim said, "I will fulfill it if I have to cut his tongue out in the City of Mexico."

Me and Tom and the two Smiths rode over to learn about the killing, and found out that the noted horse and cattle thief had done this. His name was San Tigo, he being the leader, with three gamblers in Matamoros as companions. They were the ones who killed Morgan. I said the Smiths should get Tigo and me and Tom would get the others. So we bade Sutton's wife adieu, and went to the ranch.

After getting back everything was all right. Akers, the manager for both of us, said things could not be better, and said the cattle and horses could be in no better condition. Then we got our shooting arms in fine order, and after dinner rode well mounted to Matamoros. Jim Smith and Frank went to one part to lodge and me and Tom to another, close to the side where the gambling den was located.

We arrived some time during the night, and put up our horses and pulled off our spurs and left them with the man who took care of our horses. We went to bed and slept until morning. We got up and ate breakfast and then went downtown. Met the Smith brothers but we never spoke. We prowled around town all day and when night came we were glad, for we wished to look up the gambling dens. After supper was over we went to the gambling dens. We had about a hundred dollars apiece, and left the other with a friend. We went to the house to

locate them, but failed. We thought we would stay
around and watch them play monte and other
games, but found out but little.

Next night was the same. We played cards, and
won a lot of money. Me and Tom were sitting
around another place which we thought was the
one. There was two men behind the bar who
owned it. There came in a Mexican drunk, who
stood them a round and asked, "How would you
like to kill another Gringo at the Sutton ranch?"
They only laughed. Me and Tom acted as though
we never heard them, but got up in a few minutes
and began to buck at Monte. We left after twelve,
after losing some money. The Mexicans only
smiled to think they were the winners. We went to
the hotel and Tom said we had them. The ones that
own this is a Mexican captain and a major. We had
better kill them at once. I said, "No, we must find
out how the Smith boys are getting along. The
Mexican that was drunk gave this away. We will
have to kill him on the street somewhere and then
work on the others later."

We went to see the Smith boys and formed our
plans. The Smith boys said they had not located
Tigo, but had found his chum and knew he was
close. I asked them if we had better do all the killing the same night and then leave. Jim Smith said,
"No, when you get a good chance do your killing

and go to the ranch and wait for us, and we will do the same."

Then me and Tom got our horses and put on our spurs and leggings, and went to the dive where we always visited, after getting those fellows located. We played some and stood around a great deal. The night passed very slowly and about twelve-thirty we went to the hotel, for there were too many at the gambling den to do anything that night.

We went back the next night and the drunken man would come in and go out before twelve. Me and Tom went to our inn. I said to Tom, "We never want to go there together again, and that Mexican he leaves early so we had better not kill them all together. One wants to follow the one that comes in drunk, and when he gets in a dark place try to cut his head off with a knife." We went back again. I left Tom in the dive and watched the way the Mexican went. We went back the next night and he went out as usual. Tom followed, and when he got in a dark alley Tom cut his throat and leaving his knife, came back. We played cards until late and left towards daylight. Tom said we had better blow out the lights of these and go. The Mexican was found dead, but they never did suspect us, thinking we were in the house when he left. We prowled the streets for the Smith boys and found them in a dive and had a long talk with them. We told them one had bitten the dust and the other would soon go. Jim Smith says, "Do your killing, and go to the ranch and wait for us, and if we do our killing first, we will go to the ranch and wait for you, as we expect you to do for us."

Next night we went back and played cards until late. The crowd began to get small and we left and went home. Next night we came again but we never stayed but a few minutes. We went again and played cards until late. Then me and Tom left for a few minutes. I told Tom they had won lots of our money and when we go back you get our horses and we will shoot at the boys.

Chapter 20

KILLING OF CAPTAIN GONDALES, MAJOR DECELLI VERCIPUCI, AND WHAN DEOLI.

After me and Tom gambled a few minutes, Tom stopped and walked out, and after Tom left my luck changed and I won their money in a hurry and came very near having them broke. This I did not want to do, as I wanted Tom to get back and we would both be in it.

The Mexicans began to get mad, and I gave them some money to keep them in good humor until Tom came. I bet most anyway to lose, but won. At last they were broke again. The captain got mad and said, "You never won it fair." I said, "I did, it was you-all's game and I beat you at it, too." He again said, "You never." I said, "If you are not satisfied I will give part of the money back." I continued to talk, for I was trying to give Tom time to come.

All four of the Mexicans were around the table and as soon as Tom came in I was to open the ball, if they would wait, which I was afraid they would not do. The captain says, "We are a going to have all that money." I said, "I would like for you to try it." He made an attempt to knock out the candles and lights with a revolver, and when he had hit the first light I brought out my revolvers and shot him twice, killing him instantly. With my left hand I killed two more. The major had out his revolver and shot twice, but he never got another shot for I shot him three times before he hit the floor.

Tom came rushing in and I told him I could not wait, and was sorry, for if he had been there we would not have let them get a shot. We took all the money we could and mounted our horses and crossed the Rio Grande, and went to the upper ranch.

Well, I will tell about the Smith boys. They prowled around the town, and Sutton's wife told them Tigo was in town. After Jim had a talk with this woman he went to see Frank, who was sitting with his head in a pillow and his feet above his head watching the Mexicans pass. "Let us go over to that gambling den, over yonder, I feel as though there is going to be powder burnt tonight." Jim says, "I feel funny," and Frank said he knew him of old and when he spoke of such the devil was always to pay, and, if these Mexicans bother us tonight, we will make them wish they had not.

They went over to the gambling house. They were playing right and left. They went in. It was a common thing to see Americans in town, for miners, ranchmen, and cowboys came to spend the winter months. Matamoros was in full blast. Streets were lighted bright, men around the gambling tables, troubles would arise and sometimes knives were used. It took the boys but a few minutes to see everyone present. Seeing no one they were looking for and getting wearied of standing they said, "Let us go over to the Fandango," to which they both agreed. They had no trouble in getting in, and the music was so nice that the boys were soon out with a partner apiece.

Jim got a girl in a corner talking to her, and Frank noticed them watching his brother. Frank said, "Look out Jim, I see them watching and pointing at you. There is going to be fun." Jim said, "There is." He thought Frank was mistaken, for he was having such a good time he did not want to be disturbed. Frank said, "Jim, we are going to have trouble here." Then Jim only laughed, for when a man lives by the sword there is no fear when they have to do some shooting. "If they want to fight us we want it to happen in the ballroom." All at once the greasers gave a whistle, and told the women to get out, and then blockaded the door, and after Jim and Frank used up the contents of about six revolvers, there were twenty-one Mexicans down. As soon as they cleared the front door they went a back way, and got their horses and made their escape.

The Mexicans surrounded the house, but it was quite a while before they would look inside. When they did they were disappointed, and made a rush to where they kept their horses, but were too late. Frank said to Jim, "When I went in that ballroom I never dreamed it would turn out to be a slaughter pen, did you, son?" "No, but it did just the same."

They rode on and crossed the Rio Grande and got to the ranch about one-thirty and called me and Tom off and told us their failure. We told them what we had done. Jim said there may be another day.

In a day or so some Mexicans tried to steal some of our cattle, but four of the boys relieved them of the cattle and killed all but four, who escaped across the Rio Grande. The next day I and Tom went up the river and shot two Indians who were trying to steal some of our horses, and later I shot four from the brush. The Smith boys rode down the river and coming on a bunch of Mexicans with some of our cattle, fired a few shots and ran them off. The Mexicans came back again. Jim rode back to see, and found he was not mistaken. He drew his rifle and shot down eight, and the others left in a hurry. Coming up to Frank, the latter said "How did you make it with the boys?" He said, "All right. I guess I shot down eight men and nine horses." By that time another bunch of men was in sight, and Frank said, "I will go and see who they are." He found them to be United States soldiers. Frank told them how the Mexicans tried to rob and steal our cattle. The soldiers captured those who had not crossed the Rio Grande, after driving back the cattle and coming on to the ranch. So we were not afraid of an Indian invasion.

Frank and Jim began to make preparations to go to Matamoros. The firearms were all prepared. Jim said he was bound to have Tigo, so he began to get restless to go. We put him and Frank in disguise.

Chapter 21

WE MAKE ANOTHER TRIP TO MATAMOROS. JIM SMITH SAVES A GIRL'S LIFE.

The boys disguised me and Tom, after which we all rode close to the Rio Grande, and then it began to get dark. Jim and Frank stopped at an old Mexican's. Me and Tom went well mounted into Matamoros and put up at a different inn than before. Frank and Jim stopped at the Soyos. Next morning they surprised an American tiger about to spring on one of his girls, but Jim roped and dragged it to death, and they went back with the girl so she would be in no danger. This had a great influence on the old man, and he wanted the boys to stop often. The boys told him when convenient they would be glad to do so. The girl's name was Ida, and she had a half-sister whose name was Asada, who was part English.

The Smith boys told the old Soyos that they were in disguise. He said that was all right. Just then up rode Tom Scott. He had been visiting Asada. De Soyos showed them a room and gave orders for the guard to let them in, and for the peon to care for the horses at any time they should come. He made them promise to come again soon. They bade him adieu, and called off Scott and asked him what he was doing there. He said he was foolish about Asada. They told him he was smart to like her, if he went on looks. They asked him how long he was going to stay there. Scott said about an hour, and would go from here to Matamoros. They told him to say nothing about who they were. He said he would tell nothing. So telling him bye-bye, they went on to Matamoros.

When they arrived there they put up their horses and went downtown. She was in full bloom, and there was a promise of a fine day. They then prowled around until night, when they went to a gambling den, but they never found the murderer, San Tigo. Next day they ran on me and Tom, and asked how our luck was and we told them not good. We said we had Tigo in our recollections, but had failed to see him. Jim Smith said, "As soon as I see him I am going to shoot him if he's in the city of Monterrey." I told Jim it was the best not to be too rapid. Jim said anyone could not be too rapid for him. Jim said we should meet at a certain gambling house, and see if we had learned any-thing more, and said he had located his chum and knew he was close. Me and Tom talked the matter over and concluded it was not safe for us to prowl together.

The next morning he went downtown alone and I did also. I ran on Jim Smith next morning and he asked me to show him Tigo. I told him I would if he would promise not to shoot him in day time. He said, "No, I will not shoot the old scoundrel until the proper time." We walked without success from one place to another and I pointed out a Mexican whom I had seen twice with him, so Smith would know him. Smith said, "If I can do no better I will follow him some day."

I told Jim if his and Frank's money run short we would rob a gambling den. Jim said we would have to gamble to keep down suspicion. I also told him of my and Tom's luck. He said, "I know a place where we can get a boodle." So we ran around to see if we could find Tom and Frank, but failed. I went down to supper with Jim, and in a minute Tom and Frank walked in. They told us they had found out nothing and that a certain gambling out-fit had received over ten thousand in gold.

We decided to disguise ourselves and have a sham battle and make off with the money. Jim said we would go to the place at a late hour, as at that time there were very few out.

We began to fix our disguises differently, and when night came on we tied our horses close together, and began to monkey around town. After a while we went to this den to wait until the people began to leave, but they began to increase in number instead of getting smaller. So us boys went and had our horses taken care of. Me and Tom went to our room and went to bed and the Smith boys to theirs. We arose late and prowled around town until night, and then we went to see the Smith boys. Jim said we should never take our horses again. We can kill everything, scatter, and they will never know who did it. Anyway we can try it. We went to one place and then another. Tom gambled and got into a dispute and knocked a Mexican down with his fist. Then we left this part and went to another. It seemed to be an unusually dull night, for very few were on the streets. They stayed at the boarding houses.

We all had a talk and Jim Smith said, "This is our night. Let us all scatter and go where that money is, and when I whistle we will scatter and go to shooting, and after that is over we will go to our boarding place, if best." So we came in at different times and commenced to play monte. All four of the Mexicans were around the table. Jim gave a whistle and at the same time covered the Mexicans with two revolvers and said, "I want the key to the front door." We had out our revolvers by this time. Jim still told them in Mexican, after the front and back doors were locked, that he wanted the key to a certain small room. After this was done they were relieved of their firearms and locked up. Jim knew the place and knew it was the one for safe-keeping.

After the Mexicans were locked up we took all the money, which amounted to over nine thousand, which we divided.

Me and Tom went to our boarding place and the Smith boys went to the old Soyos, and returned next night. They went to a gambling den, and, after staying there a while, they noticed a cowboy gambling, who was none other than Tom Scott. So Jim and Frank walked up to him. The boys had seen a Mexican from behind making signs, which the cowboy knew nothing of. Scott had bet all his money and lost. The Mexican showed his cards as proof. At that moment Jim stuck a knife through them and said, "Scott, I am ashamed of you to let these scoundrels cheat you in such a way." He and Frank put the money in their pockets, and the Mexicans reached for their knives and revolvers. Jim and Frank covered them and said, "Drop your hands or we will kill everything." Jim said to Scott, "Come, time to go," and when they came out they met me and Tom.

So we all got on our horses and left. Me and Tom went to the ranch and the other boys to the old

Soyos. While on our way we asked Scott where he was going and he said to the old Soyos' place. Jim said, "We will go together." Frank said Scott was in love with Asada, and the other one loved him too. "Yes," said Scott, "I was trying to give all my attention to Asada, but the other one fell in love with me." Frank said, "Go ahead and tell us all about it, you don't have to explain, for it is getting so I wish to hear." "Look out," said Jim, "too many strings, and only two may be too many for you." "Yes," said Scott, "that man I was playing cards with was with the other girl, for I have seen them in the field together. I hope they are not planning against me and the girl I love so well." "No," said Jim, "I am in hopes that it is not against you, as you want to stay here. We are like wild geese and may have to travel." The Soyos liked us pretty well.

Well, me and Tom went on to the ranch and had a talk about Jim being so reckless. Tom said he is so bad he would just as soon rob the president of Mexico as not. The last words we heard Jim say were that he never came here after girls and did not intend to take any away. He was after San Tigo. He had said, "I am going to cut that tongue out of his head before I leave Mexico, and I expect him to be alive when I do it. Scott, take that girl and run away with her, kidnap or do something else and don't be slow. That other one, if you keep going there to see Asada, will kill you both or have it done, and if she cannot get you she will rejoice to burn you alive."

Chapter 22

THE SMITH BOYS AND SCOTT ARRIVE AT THE DE SOYOS. JIM SMITH GOES TO THE HORSE RACES AND THE BULL FIGHTS.

Yonder are the lights. Out came the dogs a yelping. The guard lets them in and takes their horses, and the old Soyos came out and said he was glad to see them. He then ordered the peon cook to give the boys a lunch. Scott's girl is there. The old Soyos insisted on them coming in and having a talk. The other girl had gone to town to attend the gatherings. Scott's girl is so pretty, and the outlaws said, "No wonder he fell in love with her." The cowboys were well contented now, and before retiring they all took a smoke with the de Soyos. Jim said, "I am thinking of going to town tomorrow again, and asked old Soyos if he thought he could rig him up so he would look like a Mexican. Soyos, thinking it a joke, said it would be impossible. Frank said he wanted to go but Jim said, "I would rather go alone." Then they all retired for the night, but it soon passed away, for we were weary.

After we left Scott and the Smith boys, we went on to the Rio Grande. It was during the night and we found the waters very high. So we staked out horses and slept until next day about ten. I awoke and aroused Tom. Just then a deer came in sight and I shot and killed it. We had broiled venison for breakfast and dinner also. After we had eaten our lunch we felt like English lords after a Christmas dinner. After dinner we put some meat on our saddles, because we wished to kill no more going to the ranch, for we did not wish to take the time.

We saddled our horses and prepared to ford the river. We went above where the crossing was and were about to ford when up rode five Mexicans. They were guards, and asked us where we were going. We told them to our ranch. They said they had orders not to let anyone pass, as there had been four, supposed to be Americans, who had been doing some killing at Matamoros, and also said one time they broke up a Mexican ball, and were supposed to have killed four Mexicans in a gambling house; and the same four, disguised, robbed another gambling house. So they had orders to let no one pass. We talked there quite a while to go, but they would not let us. I leaned over in my saddle. This meant for Tom to get ready, for we would try them a round. They asked us where we were from. We told them from Matamoros. We had not more than got the last word out when we had two of them dead, and by the time the others had out their revolvers we had them all down. One was not quite dead and he begged hard for his life, but I told Tom it would never do to leave one alive, so his brains were blown out.

After the killing we shot down all the Mexicans' horses, so they could not be seen very far. We then forded the Rio Grande and went to the ranch. We got there towards night. Everything was in a flourishing condition. There was a cattle buyer from Galveston who wanted to buy three thousand steers, so me and Tom sold him that many and made a roundup and delivered them, and then had a couple of the boys see them out of the range, so they would get no more cattle. Me and Tom sat around and watched the boys ride broncho horses. We paid them all the money due them when the cattle were sold.

Well, I will tell about Jim Smith's trip back to the city next day. The old Soyos and Frank put a captain's rig on him, and everything was so complete he was a sure Mexican in disguise. They said, "What name are you going by?" He said, "Captain de Donahoo." His horse was saddled with an officer's saddle, and when it was ready he mounted and rode to Matamoros. So many strange people came to this place, no attention was paid to him. This was the day for the bull fights and the horse races, and the town was crowded. Having learned the way, he turned his horse and went with the crowd. Jim wondered if San Tigo would be present. Jim knew he was a fellow who took a great part in such sports, and always came and went at pleasure. The bull fight was about to come off. So James left his horse in a good place and went to a location where he would be liable to see the man he wanted. The fight began, and one horse was hooked and another was killed. The next one they came very near not killing, but one Mexican put a spear in his neck and from the loss of blood he soon fell.

Jim, as well as watching the fight, was looking for Whan de Foyo and San Tigo. Soon up walked de Foyo, but he did not stay. Jim watched the fight, but soon left and went to a gambling outfit, who were betting on shooting a sage hen, a duck, and a turkey. The captain walked up and was looking on when de Foyo, Tigo's friend, said, "Let the captain shoot." Jim was only watching the movements of the fowls. They wanted the captain to see if he could hit the fowls' heads, as so many had failed. They kept on annoying him until Jim said he would if they would let him use his own revolver, which they agreed upon. It was a dollar a shot, and the one who hit the sage hen was to get seventy-five dollars, the turkey fifty, and the duck twenty-five. Jim, having paid his three dollars, pulled out a long revolver, and when he did this they called him a certain lieutenant. Jim looked at his revolver to see if she was all right. All at once three shots were heard, and up walked the lieutenant for his money. All the fowls had lost their heads. The money was given without a word. The Mexicans yelled for him. Jim then walked away, but not out of sight, for he was watching de Foyo, and knew Tigo was not far off. It was now dinner time. De Foyo mounted his horse and so did Jim. Jim put his horse close to this man and went to the same place to get his dinner. The Mexicans did not see him, so he got a room where he could see the dining table and also the street. Out came de Foyo, for his dinner. Up walked a Mexican. "Where away?" said de Foyo.

"I am hunting some of our men."

"Stop and sit down."

"Me have no time to talk to you. Haven't much time and have to go "

"What is your rush?"

"I know a lot."

"Sit down and tell me."

"Those gringos."

"What," says de Foyo, "They are here again?"

"Two were followed to the Rio Grande."

"Where did the other two go?"

"Me tell you after while."

"Have something to drink?"

"After they got to the Rio Grande they killed five Mexican guards and went on to Texas. The other two stopped at the Soyos, for they are great friends, as one of those fellows saved his girl's life. He thinks there is no one like them."

"I will kill them yet," said de Foyo.

"And one of those fellows, disguised as a Mexican officer, came to this town this morning."

"The great thunder, he was at the bull fight, and shot three fowls' heads off and carried away a lot of money. If I had only known this I would have killed him."

Jim Smith heard all of this and could have killed them but thought it best to wait.

"Who told this?" asked de Foyo.

"One of the girls at the Soyos, who wanted San Tigo to do her a favor some way, and wanted him to keep quiet. I know not the secret."

Jim said to himself, "Scott, Tom, you had better look out."

De Foyo said, "Let us have every place searched for that fellow disguised as a Mexican officer, and his horse also."

Jim was in trouble about that girl. He then came out to dinner, as the Mexicans had passed his horse and he felt safe. After dinner was over he bought some clothes and changed his dress, and put the officer's rig under some bed clothes and left them for good. Then Jim prowled around town. One time he met de Foyo but never acted as if he had seen him. Jim said the next place he went to was a dry goods house, but he did not purchase anything. From there he went to a small store and bought a pair of boots. The Mexican told him if he wished to try them on he should go to a dark corner in the back of the house. Jim went to the back part and was thinking of the way the Mexicans were wanting to kill them.

All of a sudden two men walked back, and one said, "I was going to tell you about that gold and silver train. It will be along in five days. The fourth day we want to go to the old Soyos and then to this gold train. We can then say it was those Texas cattlemen who did the work. If we can kill that Smith gang we will have no more trouble. But, did you ever see such men come in our town, kill our people, and us not know them?"

"Never you mind," says the other, "we will kill them and cut their heads off. Where will this robbery take place?"

"Oh, it will be at the bluffs of the canyon as they will stop there that night for water. I don't think there's water close to those small lakes, and we will kill all and take the gold. I will talk to you again about this." So they left.

After they had gone Jim put on his boots and walked around town. Night was coming on and he wanted to find Tigo. Jim found out from a certain Mexican that San Tigo had a gambling den in a certain part of town. Jim asked the greaser if they dealt monte. The Mexican said, "Yes," "Let us go down," said Jim. So Jim and the Mexican went down and bet on monte.

Chapter 23

SAN TIGO COMES IN AND JIM GETS A GOOD LOOK AT HIM.

After Jim and the Mexican played monte quite a while, in walked a Mexican, well dressed. The Mexican ran and shook hands with him, and called him Master Tigo. Smith knew this was his man, but acted as though he had never seen him, but kept on playing his monte. In a short while he left and went to supper, after which he went downtown.

Later on he got his horse and rode out to the Soyos' home. He found Frank and Scott asleep, as it was late when he got in. He gave the guards his horse, and went to bed without arousing anyone. The peon aroused them for breakfast and after breakfast Jim and Frank saddled their horses. Jim said, "Scott, I want to speak to you." He told him what he had found out and that one of the old Soyos' girls had told where they had been hiding. And Jim said, "Scott, you had better take that girl and leave, or they will kill you." Scott seemed to be in trouble.

Jim and Frank started for the ranch, but they had not gotten far before a crowd of Mexicans from Monclova, who were drunk, began to follow them and fired off revolvers. The reason they did this was they wished to frighten the boys, but to their disappointment it did not have the desired effect. When they were about a hundred yards near, the boys took their revolvers and shot the first two dead, and before the others could get away they had two more down. By this time the others were at full speed. So the Smith boys left four Monclova Mexicans dead. These Mexicans were very dangerous they thought, and were on their way to join Tigo's band. These Mexicans had had so many people run from them they were surprised at these two fellows. But it took a larger crowd to make the Smith boys run. After this happened the boys rode for the Rio Grande, and coming up to this river, four Mexicans stopped them and told them they would not let them pass, for some white people disguised as Mexicans were wanted at Matamoros. Without another word the Smiths shot all four down, and leaving their horses so the other Mexicans could find and bury them, they rode on to the ranch, getting in about dark. We had not gone to bed, so when they came in we gave them supper.

After supper they came in where me and Tom and the cowboys were. I asked them if they had had any trouble at the Rio Grande. Frank said, "No, I guess the Mexicans had the trouble." They asked us how we came out. We told them we left five men and as many horses dead. I asked them how many did they get and they said four. We sat up late and talked cattle business, and before we went to bed there came a man who wished to stay all night. The boys asked us and we told him he could. I told the cowboys to show him a place to put his saddle and horse.

Frank said, "I have heard, I believe, that voice before." It seemed that way to me, but I have heard so many in the past.

And after his horse was attended to he came in. Frank said, "I thought I knew that voice."

Jim came in and said, "I am acquainted with him."

Jim asked, "Where in the thunder are you going?" He said, "We will all go together, and that soon. You are in no hurry, I suppose."

"No, I am glad to see you all. How long have you been in this country?"

"Quite a while," said Frank, "and if you will wait a while we will go to Mexico and have a hot time, like the days in Missouri, from sixty-one to sixty-five. Let me make you acquainted with one of my guerrilla friends, who was with us during the war. You can trust him as far and also in any place."

Tom asked him if he had been to supper and he said, "No." Tom ordered the cook to get him something to eat. Frank asked, "Where did you go after the war?"

"I went in the cattle trade in the northern part of the Indian Territory, close to the southern part of Kansas. Me and some of the men did some killing and I sold out and left. Then I went to St. Louis and spent most of my money, and with what I had left came to Galveston, and from there here, by way of Corpus Christi, and buying a horse at the last place started to Mexico this way. I heard of this ranch and came by. How is it you boys came to this country?"

"To get a rest, and so they would not hunt us like bears." "Did any of them ever come here to hunt you?"

"Yes, one of Mr. Pink's men came to see us and asked for work."

"Did you give him work?"

"Yes, we put him on the river," and then Frank winked at him. "We always have work for them."

"Dave Pool is in Arizona."

"Yes, it has been quite a while since I heard from any of the boys we used to be with."

"Will Anderson, another one of Quantrell's men, is in the Indian Territory. He has a lot of indictments against him." "How many do you suppose?" "About a hundred."

"Well, he has enough to do him."

"How do you like the ranch life?"

"Pretty well, we want to see Missouri again."

"I am proud you came, we need you in our line of work."

"Who are these fellows with you?"

"They are Yanks, and they arc birds. We have laid down the Stars and Bars and the Stars and Stripes, and are working under the Mexican flag now. You should go to the Mexico precincts with us. We have been painting that side red. We have a great deal more fun than in the Civil War. We think as little of killing a Mexican or an Indian as we would a jack rabbit."

Frank did the talking. It was getting time for us to retire, which we did, and the night passed away pleasantly.

Frank called us up the next morning and asked what name our visitor went by. He said, "You all call me Jack Lewis. Don't call me by my correct name in Missouri, for they will locate me." After breakfast, when all the men had gone to look after the horses and cattle, with the exception of one we had sent to Fort Brown to get our mail, we began to tell Lewis what we had done for the Mexican lads. Frank was a great talker and wanted to tell his friend all the news.

"We robbed," Frank said, "a Mexican gold train, taking the horses, mules, and all the money. We went to Texas and had a fine time, and when we get short we go to Mexico and take on a supply. I will tell you, Lewis, how we came to have so many cattle. We came here with but a small number to start with, and us Yanks and Rebs fell in love with one another. These Mexicans began to steal cattle from Texas and kill the owners and their cowmen. After they had done their work above and crossed about twenty miles us boys had a talk and said that was a picnic for us. So we prepared to go in the cattle business on a large scale. There were three or four of these herds from Texas, driven by these Mexican thieves and cutthroats, who had killed the owners and the cowboys, and were on their way to Mexico. We captured these herds, and killed all the Mexicans. So you see we have gone in the cattle business on a large scale, investing nothing but powder and lead, and of course we lost a little sleep.

"Tom and Hale robbed a gambling den, killed four, and got a nice lot of money. All of us robbed another and had three or four fights on the river."

Jim said, "Frank you have talked long enough. To make a long story short, Lewis, we are about to rob another gold train – silver in it also. Will you help us, will you go?"

"I will do nothing else but go."

"When we rob this we will divide the money. There is a Mexican we want to kill, who murdered a friend of ours, a near ranchman, and then said us Texas cattlemen did it." Lewis said, "I want to see him now."

Jim said, "This Mexican is going to kill the men with the gold and silver train, and get possession and then we are going to kill them. Then the gold and silver will be in our possession." Frank said we wanted to be like a certain lawyer, in a picture, who was milking a cow. Two men got in a dispute over her. One was pulling her by the horns and the other by the tail and the lawyer was milking her. One of the men pulled off the horns and the other the tail. The lawyer was through, so he drove her off. We want to be like the lawyer and carry off the boodle, at the last.

Tom said to Lewis, "The leader of these Mexican robbers is named San Tigo. We call him Tigo for short, and Jim wants to tongue him for killing Sid Sutton." Jim said first we want to get everything ready, our firearms in fine working order, and a mule loaded with provisions. At that moment the cook called us to dinner. After dinner the man came with the mail from Fort Brown, and there was a letter from father wanting me to sell out and come and live with him. It said that country must be lonesome to a young fellow of my age. This gave me a great many unpleasant thoughts and brought things to my memory of the past life. I said I may go soon. I am about ready to leave anyway.

About the middle of the evening we mounted our horses to go to that silver and gold train. We traveled a long way and when we came to the canyon, we camped for the night. The next day we stayed where we were on account of the grass being so fine for our horses, and it was but a short way to where we could see them coming in the canyon. We took time to watch for them, and after dinner took our horses to water and moved closer.

Chapter 24

THE FIGHT CLOSE TO THE CANYON. PALAMETHO AND MANY A MEXICAN CHEWS THE DUST.

It was Tom's turn to watch and when hc was out about half an hour he said, "I see them coming." We all went out and waited until they came in plain view. There were eighteen mule drivers and as many soldiers. James said before the night passes away many a one is to die. Frank said, "Lewis, what do you think about it?" Lewis said, "I wish we were ready now, and I am in hopes we will not have to wait so long." Jim said, "This makes Lewis think of the days in Missouri."

"Yes, Lewis is thinking of some things that happened in Missouri. All of this must happen before daylight."

Jim said, "I see the captain. I wish I knew how many men Tigo is going to have, but I guess I will have to have patience and wait and see." Jim said, "There are going to be a great many against us this night, unless there are lots of San Tigo's men killed." Jim said, "There are only five of us, but we want that money." He said we could kill this gold train, but we want the others to do that and save us the trouble. We can kill the others at the last. Jim said, "I presume the gold train we captured before told these to be careful and let no strangers travel with them, and it made the government think more guards were needed." It made no difference, for we had planned to have it, and we wanted it. To our surprise the train stopped on the flat country, and we began to get everything ready so nothing would be wanting.

Jim said, "If I can, I want Tigo's tongue with that plunder. I want that if I can get it, if not I can do without it." Smith said he would hate to leave Mexico without killing Tigo, for, he said, he would never die happy. It was getting dark and we must move closer. I told them we must not run into Tigo's men. "No," said Jim, "we don't want the first fight." Frank said the one that laughs last laughs the longest.

In a short while we saw lights and the camp was bright as day. I said we had better be careful if Tigo's men are on the ground, for if we get too close we will run into them. So we halted. We got to a place where Jim said we could leave our horses, and go to a place where we could watch the battle. We believe it will come off soon, and are anxious to see who whips. So Jim proposed to get to a certain place where we would be in no danger. He gave so many orders that we called him our captain, and told him to lead the way. So us four crawled along after him. It was quite a while before the place was reached. Jim knew the ground, and how the land lay, and could take us to the small elevation needed, so we could see the battle. Several times we found ourselves close to the Mexicans and had to come to a check. Jim said, "Good San Tigo and his men are here early, and must be aware the camp will be hard to take. This is the reason he was on the ground so early. We kept on after Jim. All at once Jim takes out his pipe and makes the sign of smoking and we could smell the pepper and tobacco burning. Mexicans are great lovers of their pepper. We heard Mexicans talking very low.

We came to a stop again, and our travel was very slow and we soon reached a place where all was safe. We then got everything ready in case Tigo's men ran onto us. We put out a picket as we did not want anything to go against us. Still we thought it was of no use to have one out, now that we were out of the way. We had gotten under some brush on a small bluff, and could see everything in their camp. We could hear them talking. Jim said in a whisper, "This is the only place we can see the camp, and we will see who has the gold and silver." We crept from under the brush and looked at them. We were in no danger unless a stray bullet should come our way, and when we looked at them we could see them arrange their camp. The horses and mules were hobbled out and a few tied up. Guards had been placed all around the camp so it would be difficult to surprise them.

The camp was in a fine location, offering advantages and defenses and would be hard to take. Jim said, "They have stopped at the place wanted. After the horses were cared for, the Mexican mule drivers and soldiers sat around the fire, telling yarns, smoking and some eating. They seemed to take the world easy. This is always the way with a Mexican if he gets all he wants to eat and smoke and plenty of rest. The guards were watchful and thought they were safe, but they did not know that some other Mexicans were waiting for them. Oh, there were some bad things yet to happen. It would be sad to some, but not to San Tigo, or the ones who were waiting to have battle with Tigo. There had been nothing seen of Tigo's men, since we had taken our position. He probably was going to keep quiet until he had his men all in their places selected by their leader. Us ranchmen watched with eagerness for the ball to open. When it does we will see fun, and how it will end is uncertain.

The soldiers and the others began to go to bed, except one lazy man who was asleep by the camp fires, as soon as the preparations were over, and the camp would soon be quiet. We saw two who were not on guard looking at the horses and mules to see if they had been properly cared for, after which they came in and went to bed. By a tree and some bushes the gold and silver, which we hoped to have in our possession soon, was hidden. We wanted to take it across the river and divide. We also saw one tent stretched, which was so pretty we supposed it was for the commander.

It is but a short while before he is seen going from one guard to another, talking to them and making motions and seemed to be giving them instructions. Us lads saw this and it brought a smile over our faces. Lewis said the other Mexican is going to have a hard time taking this by storm, if he is not careful. Jim said he would come ahead to locate and get ready, so he can carry it easy. I said he was a good one if he takes it that easy. After the commander had talked to all the guards he went to his tent to bed, thinking nothing will go wrong.

Twenty minutes had passed and we are satisfied that Tigo and his men are coming on slowly. We are guessing that it will happen soon, for San Tigo had them located, and his men obey his instructions. I am satisfied that the scout saw them talking and smoking, and telling their yarns.

We became wearied. Lewis said, "I am getting anxious for the ball to open."

Jim said, "Keep quiet, it will soon begin, and when Tigo gives the order the bullets will whistle, and the excitement run high. And this will come to pass soon."

But what about ours? Lewis said, "I wish we were ready now. It is so bad to wait, but better late than never. There will be little sleep this night unless it is forever."

Jim said, "Look quick, there comes a man on that guard, and the guard standing closest to him looks sleepy. I presume he had forgotten what his commander had told him. And this will soon be his last as Tigo has selected him."

Lewis said, "Look, it will soon begin, and we all had better see it." And at the renegade's order several more came in view. He seemed to tell them something, and pointed to other parts, and some went away. When the other ones had gone he looked at the camp no longer, for he had seen everything he wished to see.

The guard thought there was no danger, but when he turned and looked toward the camp of men, old Tigo takes aim with his rifle, and we soon see the smoke and hear the report. The guard screams and drops his gun, and tries not to fall, but soon does. We hear other guns and Lewis said that means the death of those other guards, and when he sent those men off they were to kill the other guards. The signal had been given and there will be many who go to their end.

It has been a little light so we could see what they were doing. Several of the gold train had been killed. We saw them firing from different sides, and now and then one of Tigo's men is killed. Four or five charge the train but are shot down. "Good," says Jim, "we want lots of his men killed as he has too many anyway." Two more attempt to steal some of the silver but are cut down. Tigo jumped in and cut one to pieces with his knife. Jim said, "This dog had killed many a one this way, and he is not going to let any get away." How it will end we cannot tell. We are anxious for it to close so we can see how many of Tigo's men had been killed.

San Tigo knows that one after another will fall until the others will run for their lives. A great number are killed on both sides, and we are glad. There may be others dead in the brush, as the bullets have been hissing. We praise the bravery of the train. There were so many of them killed, and if it keeps on accordingly, it will be easy for us. We still see the battle raging and we are glad. Every once in a while one goes to the ground, never to rise again. We can tell who is going to win the battle.

At the first the commander came out and gave orders, and guided his men. Tigo and his men retire and are shooting at long range. It seems that the crew who are with the gold train are good marksmen, and their commander was brave. The Mexicans tried to kill him in preference to the others, which does not alarm him, for he comes out and gives orders. He keeps away from the fires, which is very wise of him, for as soon as he comes out of the tent many a shot is fired at him. He knows they are in a hurry to kill him, and if he were to fall his men would lose hopes and run away, and lose everything. We could hear his voice telling his men what to do. Stand close and keep together, if not they would all be killed.

We are satisfied his men knew the worst had not come yet. We think the battle is not going to last long at this rate, for they will charge soon. Tigo and his men will make a rush and end the battle. We see the commander keep close and not expose himself. He is no fool, as he has arranged his men so they can no longer shoot them from long range. Frank said, "I would like to know when this will come to an end. Unless these Mexicans make a different movement, it will not close until night. They have not done so much damage, even though there has been many killed." The firing ceases and voices are heard. This is for San Tigo and his men to get closer, and close in. Lewis said there is something else on the program, they are planning to kill all. Frank said, "It will not end before the light appears in the east, as they are night crows, and I am in hopes they will make a rush and a lot more get killed." A lot of wood is thrown on the fires, as they want them kept up, so if they would come in camp to steal the gold and silver they would shoot them down. Every now and then a man is dodging and a gun fires, but very seldom doing any damage. Once in a while we hear a scream, and we know the gold boys are hitting them. The commander gets uneasy as they are getting closer instead of getting away.

San Tigo had arranged a cunning trick. His idea was to get the men to expose themselves and then kill every man. All the while he kept track of the commander and where he was hiding. Then we saw some of his men make a mock attack on the lower side of the camp. The commander of the treasure train made a rush for this part, as they expected the robber and his men to come from that part. He thought this was the place to defend, and he gave the order for his men to go to this place where they were threatened. This was a fatal mistake on their part for the other side was waiting for them to expose themselves. They had their guns ready for the deadly work. As soon as they heard the guns on their rear they saw their mistake. It was too late now to change his plans. He now rushed forward to defend those in front and to die brave. His men were scared to death by the firing in their rear, and if they had been as brave as their commander they would have kept San Tigo guessing. He saw his men go down all around him.

A dozen or more managed to reach the place where their friends were fighting for their lives, and the commander and the new men put courage in their minds. Their rush was so great that it looked as though they were going to gain. They were shooting the robbers down right and left, and the robbers were killing a good many of them.

Now they are in the light of the fires so we can see them plainly. The mule drivers fight with great bravery and are all together now. Jim said, "I was glad they did not go in those brakes to camp, for I knew they would kill a lot of the robbers." And as long as the commander can be seen by his men they will fight, no matter how large the force is against them. By the robbers' actions they were aware of this. He and his men are fighting for life. The robbers make a rush for the commander, Tigo and his men double their efforts to kill him, but he seems to have a charmed life and cannot be hit with lead. Several of Tigo's men knew this and rushed for him. We think his time is short now. The captain, or commander, will go soon, and he knows it. Every time he turns he meets blows aimed for his life. He could get away, but he don't do such, but goes down like a brave mother with her child. Even we above watch this with great sorrow. They soon see it is all over, their commander being killed by someone behind him. His last attempt was to kill the one that shot him, with his sword, which he did. He goes to the ground never to rise again. As soon as his men see him fall they run for their lives, and the murderers are glad they go. The treasure had been defended at a terrible cost and with great bravery. They throw down their arms and rush for the valley, and by the next night reach Matamoros and tell of the slaughter and robbery.

These outlaws have proved that they can fight if they do boast. This canyon battle is over with the Mexicans and some gringos will next appear. Just then four more of the gold train come out from another place and begin to fight, killing a number of the robbers. Jim said, "There is old Tigo in it again." They are shooting right and left and have killed all but one who is being fired at rapidly. Just then a gun was fired among our crowd, and looking around I found that Jim Smith was the one. I asked him if he fired on purpose and he said, "No." I asked, "What in the thunder do you mean, Jim, don't you know that they will locate us and it will be difficult to get the gold?" Jim said, "No, I have kept count and there is only twelve left alive. They will think that these are the ones who made their escape." Just then another gun was fired by Lewis. I said, "You all are in a hurry." At that moment Frank and Tom fired, and I also took aim and another went over the road. This only left a few of the robbers.

They never thought that another enemy was at hand, and it was as Smith said, they would think nothing about us. They must have thought that the ones we had killed were from the shots in the battle. Now they think that they have possession and prepare to stay there the rest of the night. The fires are made brighter by putting on more wood. Jim said, "I see them carrying old Tigo in his or in the commander's tent." He also said, "I aimed to shoot and break his back, so I can cut his tongue out and show it to him when he is alive."

We still watch the camp, and, after Tigo is taken in the tent, we hear a great noise. They are getting everything located. The robbers placed a guard over the silver and gold. Jim said, "I am so happy that there was water out here, so they did not go down in that canyon to camp." We continued to stay in this location, and began to get restless and change our position. Tom said he would be glad if our part was over.

Strange people seemed to be around the camp during the last hour, and inside noises were going on. We had made a discovery. Jim Smith and us decide they have prisoners. Who they are and how many we cannot tell as they are kept back from the fires. Lewis was called and relieved of his position by me. We still think it best to have out pickets. Lewis said it is a man and a woman. "By jingo," said Frank, "I will bet it is Tom Scott and Asada." Lewis was noted for his eyesight and said he was not mistaken. We can now see plainly they are kept under guard. Jim said that other girl was the cause of all of this, and they are in luck that we came to rob that train.

By the time the camp is sound asleep Jim said it is time for us to go below, for they are getting quiet now. Jim said we have seen and done all we can from this position, and we wished to see what we could do below. "Our time has come," said Lewis, "and I am happy of it." So we went down as cautiously as we came up, for the old Mexican had guards placed out and we had to be careful. At last we are at the bottom and the Mexicans are very close to us. Here Jim said, "I will leave you and see what is the best for us to do."

Chapter 25

JIM SMITH CUTS A MEXICAN SENTRY'S THROAT AND RELIEVES THEM OF THEIR CAPTIVES.

Jim goes to see who those captives are, and if they are Scott and the girl, rescue them if he can, and if possible get the Mexican leader. So Jim starts and gets the Mexican guard located. Jumping on him he cut his throat with a Mexican knife, a double-edged stiletto, after which it was no trouble for him to pass. He thought no more of killing the Mexican guard than if he'd been a jack rabbit. One more greaser to give an account for, but such dogs made no difference to him. There is no one to annoy him so he goes on. The fires are very low so that he can get around without being seen. He was anxious to locate the place where we had seen the prisoners from the heights. It was as Lewis said, a man and a woman who were prisoners, and getting near found it to be Scott and the girl.

It was a misfortune to fall into their hands. While Scott was at the Soyos' place, he did all in his power to escape, but without success, and at the time was overpowered. The cause of all this was the other girl, Ida. We found out that San Tigo abused him, and was going to wait for orders as to what should be done with them. It was my belief that the other girl was to give the orders, and they would burn or kill them. They would have disposed of them in some way. Ida disliked Scott because he loved the other one instead of her. It was lucky for them we needed that money.

Jim came up slowly and wanted no trouble until we were ready for it. At first he saw how many guards were out. He found they had only three; one was over the gold and silver, one over Scott and the girl, and another on a different side of the camp looking out on that quarter. They were quite a distance apart. From what Jim saw, it looked as if the prisoners were tied. He will have to pass the guard, who would have to be killed. The guard is well armed, has two revolvers, a knife, and a rifle in his hand. The first thing Jim did was to jump on him and cut his head almost off. He then goes to the prisoners and finds them to be Scott and the girl. After cutting them loose he came with them to us, and said, "Stay here, I am going back to kill another guard, and after that I may want the help of you all. Scott, I was expecting them to kill you all at once. How many of this man's men did get killed, Scott?"

"Almost all."

"Well," says Jim, "we will get the balance. Say, Scott, is old Tigo shot?"

"Yes, his back is broken."

"Good," said Jim, "that is where I aimed to shoot him."

Scott said, "You never shot him."

Jim said, "At the last part we all got restless and shot one apiece. I shot San Tigo and these others got envious and shot them one apiece." Scott said the leader was in that tent with one man attending him.

"Well, I will go and watch and get another guard and learn about San Tigo." So Jim said, "Lewis, you can go with me." Jim and Lewis went to see what could be done. They located the guard that was away from the camp. Jim said, "Lewis, you hide behind this rock and when he walks close you jump and cut his head off, and I will kill the one over the silver and gold." So Lewis hid behind the rock and waited, and when the guard walked up Lewis jumped on him and cut his head very nearly off. Jim said, "Come on Lewis, I have not gone to that other guard, I wanted to see you doctor him."

Jim and Lewis went where the fellow was guarding the silver and gold, first investigating to see if he was the only one up. They find that three are asleep, and two in the tent. Jim said, "I made a miscount. Ah, they have a bad number." So they go to the guard and Jim knocked him down with a dub, and proceeded to amputate his head. After this was over he came for me and Frank, leaving Lewis to guard the sleepers, and told me all were dead but five, that we should come and finish. Tom was told to stay with Scott and the girl.

"No," said Tom, "I want to go."

"Yes," said Scott, "Let him go, we are all right."

"Well," said Jim, "come on."

So we went and Jim said, "Frank, you and Tom, and also Lewis, want to kill these as soon as me and Hale get in that tent. We are going to have a fine time when we crawl under the side." So me and Jim went and raised the tent sides and looked under, and there we saw old Tigo and one man. The man was asleep. Old Tigo was suffering death from his broken back. Jim said, "Follow me," and he went under with me after him. As soon as we had gotten under we found a candle and lit it. Old San Tigo yells to his man, "Here are these ranchmen, get up and kill them." I was on him, and I had a fine knife and when I worked on him a while he caused no more trouble. At this time Jim was on Tigo and relieved him of his firearms. He yelled and screamed for the other man, but you see the other man did not hear him.

Jim said, "San Tigo, you know how you have done us Texas cattlemen and what you have said we had done, when you and your men had done it yourselves."

He said, "If you will not kill me I will never tell such again." "No," said Jim, "you will not anyway." Jim said, "Put your tongue out of your mouth." He would not. Jim ripped back his jaw and took it out, and cut it out of his mouth, and said holding it up, "This is a token of good will for the ranchman's wife you and your men murdered, and said we had done it. We will please ask you to remember it, and now to make the time short will finish you up." Jim then threw the tongue on the body, and we go out to the other boys, who said all was over. Jim said, "Let us all look and be sure."

We prowled around and found that all were dead. A few of the animals had broken loose on account of the battle, but there were plenty for our own use. We had a nice lot of gold and silver. Jim said, "Frank, go and get Scott and the girl, as we want to pack the horses and mules, for daylight will soon be here."

Lewis found they had a nice lot of provisions, which we took. Scott and the girl came and we began to make preparations to get the brutes ready. I and Tom went after the other horses, and when we got back the other boys were busy putting the

silver and gold bags on the animals. Scott had
found horses for his girl and himself. After we had
loaded our animals with something to eat we were
ready to go. Jim said, "What will we do with those
other horses?" I said, "Turn them loose." We did
and all was now ready. The balance of the horses
had been turned loose, and Jim said, "Are you all
ready to go?" So we all said we were ready, and we
started at daybreak.

When we rode a couple of miles it was light. A
little farther and the sun was up.

Jim said, "Scott, how came you to be with
them?" "Well, there came a great crowd and captured us."

"Was this all of the crowd that came to the old
Soyos' place?"

"No, this was a little over half."

"Where did those others go?"

"Tigo told them to go and do a certain robbery,
and meet him at the bluffs today."

"Well, they may follow us."

"Well," said Lewis, "if they do we will rag with
them."

Jim said, "They may follow, so we will have to
look out for the boys."

We rode on until twelve and coming to some
water stopped for dinner, and let our animals graze,
for they all seemed wearied. All went to sleep but

me and Jim Smith, as we thought it best for some one to be on the lookout.

After we had stopped here about a half hour, we aroused the others and told them it was time for us to get on the road. We arranged everything and were soon on the road.

Jim said, "I have come to the conclusion that we need a couple in advance so we will not run into anything, and we also need a couple behind, as it is my belief that they will follow." Scott says, "This was not all of the robber's men." Jim said, "Me and Lewis will lead the way, and Hale, you and Frank keep a distance behind us as they will follow." So Jim and Lewis went on. Scott, the girl, and Tom drove the animals. Me and Frank stopped behind to keep a lookout.

After we had been behind quite awhile, we noticed a Mexican following us on a Mexican mule. Frank said, "Do you suppose he is one of that crowd that Scott was speaking of?" I said, "It may be possible." He continued to follow and was careful not to get too close to us. When he came in an opening, or flat place, Frank said, "I am going to shoot his animal from under him, just for fun." So Frank took aim and the report of the gun had just died out, when the mule began to pitch and threw the Mexican and then ran away. As soon as the Mexican touched the ground he was up also and was running. "Well," says I, "I will see how close I can shoot without hitting him," so I began to smoke him. Frank said, "I will help." We threw dust all over him until be got out of range of our guns.

We then rode on, and towards night we began to think of camping for the night, as our animals were weary and we also. We unpacked when the sun went down and cooked supper. After supper all went to sleep, but one, who was to be up awhile and keep a lookout. We took the watch as our turns would come. Jim Smith was on last guard, and when the light began to appear in the east, he yelled, "Get up, it is time for breakfast." He said it was a surprise that they did not follow.

Scott said, "I am glad of it."

James said, "I don't care, we would just as soon have ragged with them again as not."

After breakfast was over Scott's girl became sick and Jim said, "We will go to his ranch and see him safe." It was because she had been in so much trouble and it was so wearisome for her. We managed to get to his ranch without any trouble, and stayed there a couple of days. We did not want to go to his ranch, as it was a long distance from ours and was not on the direct route. His three men were doing very nicely. After the first day Scott's woman began to get better, for all she needed was rest.

We began to clean up our firearms and got ready to go to our ranch. We were well rested and felt so much better. Scott's woman was up and about.

Chapter 26

THE LAST DAYS OF THE SMITH GANG. WE NEVER SEE TOM SCOTT AGAIN. WE ALL WERE GLAD TO LEAVE.

The second evening at Scott's ranch was spent in preparing to leave. A cattleman from Corpus Christi came and wanted to buy Scott's ranch, and offered him a good price. Scott sold and told us he was going to move on a small creek called the Colorado creek, a little distance north. He said he was afraid to be too close to this Mexican part. Jim said, "That is a good idea."

I went in and had a long talk with Scott's wife. She said when they got located again, we should all come on a long visit. I told her I was thinking of the north and northeastern countries again, and may leave as we had a bad reputation, for the time may be close when the United States guards on the river might be against us. She said she was sorry we thought of leaving that part of the country. I said, "It may be the best for us to go, as you know what we have done, and we have been doing something similar all the time." I told her I would have a talk with the other boys when on our way to the ranch, and if they thought it best we would go, and I may go anyway, as I think I have been here long enough.

Scott and his man closed their trade, and when this was over Jim said, "Scott, we are going to divide the gold and silver, come if you want part."

He said, "No, I don't need it."

We divided it in five equal shares, and arranged it on our pack saddles for the coming morning. When this was done we retired again and slept close to sundown. Scott's men called us for supper, after which he sat around and talked until late. Scott asked, "How came you all to be where we were?" James said, "Easy, I heard a Mexican say that the gang was going to rob this gold train, and we all thought we would rob them. I believe we like gold better than any Mexican, and think these other boys do also."

Mrs. Scott asked Jim how he liked this country. Jim said, "Pretty well, but I would like to see my old home in Missouri again. I think Old Mexico Mexicans can do without my company, if not they can send me an invitation, and if I am close I may call on the gentlemen."

I said, "I think it is in the writing for us to go."

"Well, we will talk over this tomorrow."

"Scott, did that black scoundrel kill any of the Soyos' people?"

"No," said Scott, "they seemed to want us only."

"Yes," said Jim, "That's who they wanted. Where were you when the battle was going on?"

"We were down under a bank heavily guarded."

Scott's woman asked Lewis how he liked the southern country. He said all was alike to him if he had friends in the country where he was staying. He asked, "When are you going home again?"

She said, "I cannot, as the other señorita would murder me."

Scott asked, "Are you all going to your ranch tomorrow?"

"Yes," said Jim, "if we can, but it is a long drive and ride."

"Well, it is getting time to go to bed, so we all retired, and when light came one of Scott's men aroused us for breakfast. We got up and after breakfast brought in our animals and packed them for the drive to the ranch. After we had everything ready we bade Scott and his wife good-bye. Scott's woman cried, and said she did not want us to leave as we had been such fine friends to them. If it had not been for us those people would have killed them. Frank spoke and said, "The day will come when we will all have to leave one another, and it may not be far off." We all talked awhile, and finally told them bye-bye. This is the last talk we had with Scott and was the last time we ever saw him and his wife.

We rode for the ranch. Frank was the first to begin to talk, and said, "What do you thing about Scott selling out?"

Jim said, "Only a wise thought in him, for if he would have stayed where he was they may come and murder him. The men who had escaped might come where the others had been killed and would seek to kill Scott. Some of these greasers would come over on a hunting trip and murder him."

"They might," said Lewis, "come over and stay around these sheep men until the opportunity came. What do you think about that small creek he is going to move on?"

I was the only one acquainted with that part, and I told them it was the finest of any part of the country, and my belief was he would make a big success in the cattle trade if he went to this part.

Frank asked, "Do you suppose they will say us cowmen did this killing?"

"Yes," said Jim, "they would say we did this if they knew we were at the ranch."

Lewis said, "They will say we did this and Scott would know all about it before hand."

"Yes," said Frank, "that other miss will have a great effect on those yaps."

Jim said, "Scott has a pretty woman."

Frank said, "Her sis is not ugly, if she is so infernally mean."

"How would you like to go to the Mexican part again?" asked Lewis.

I said we had better go there no more, as that whole country will be ready to murder us. I think we have no more business in that country again.

Well, we rode on, and towards dinner time came across a small lake. The grass was fine for our animals to graze on, so we stopped and unsaddled and unpacked our animals, and cooked our dinner. After dinner we stayed here about two hours, and put in our time sleeping. Of course there was one of us up all the time watching, as we thought it best to keep a man on the lookout.

We then began to get our camp things together for our drive to the ranch. If we can make it before sundown, all right, if not we will camp on the flats again. We began to ride for the ranch and we had not gone very far when we ran across some United States soldiers, who had been riding on the river. When they came up we discovered we were acquainted with some of them. They asked us which way we were driving and we quickly told them to the ranch. They asked us where we had been and we told them to Scott's ranch below, delivering cattle to some fellows. These soldiers on the river had been great friends to us before.

One asked, "Who has been selling cattle in that part?"

"Tom Scott has sold his ranch and cattle, and we have been helping him deliver."

So you see we were not telling correct news. They asked questions as usual, and wished to know what we had packed on those animals.

Jim said, "Wait, I want to talk awhile, as I have not been in the habit of keeping quiet so long, and have been in the habit of being the leader in conversations, during our ranch days together. Now, you asked what was packed on these mules. I will tell you, it is none of your infernal business. You have asked many a question and made a little fun. Now, if you are not satisfied with us we can satisfy you, and that quick. I have killed a whole herd of you blue scoundrels during the war, when I was with Quantrell. You have three to our one, but I and these men can kill you all." At this time Jim's eyes looked green. He jumped off his horse and got a handful of sand, and saying, "To show you we are not afraid of you," he pitched it in his eyes.

The leader said, "What do you mean, Jim?"

Jim said, "We mean to take no insult from anyone."

"We have been good friends to you, Jim."

"Yes, let me tell you a short story. This had better be your last time to insult us. We take nothing from anyone. How came you to come to us in such a way?"

He said, "Jim, they have accused you men of robbing, killing, and stealing."

"Yes," said Jim, "you never knew there were such liars. What did they say about the ranchman they killed, him and most of his men?"

"They said the Smith gang did it."

"We have proof that we never, for his wife was living."

"They are trying to get us to capture you all, but we don't want to."

"Yes," said Jim, "you have a fine reason, being too big cowards and have not nerve."

"Jim, we will be as good friends as before, if you will explain one thing. What did you mean by killing soldiers during the war?"

"Well I will tell you, there are three of us here who killed many in the blue. We wore blue ourselves so we would not be known. These other two were on the other side and fought against us. I was only mad when I said what I did. We are all great friends, but we want no one to insult us, when we have done you no harm. You have always been welcome at our ranch. You must all come and eat dinner, and what other meals you wish to. We have treated you all as brothers." He said, "Jim, the Mexicans dislike all of you."

Jim said, "I will tell you the reason. When they bother us they have to fight, and because they cannot handle us the way they like to they are dissatisfied."

He also said, "Jim, they want you all."

"Yes," said Jim, "tell them to come and get us. I will tell you what they want. They would like to have our cattle and horses, but we are too good with our rifles and revolvers. They would like to do us as they have some other Texas cowmen – kill us and take our cattle."

"Well," said Jim, "it is time for us to go, and the next time we will report to Fort Brown if we don't kill you all." So we rode away, and began to get our animals together to shove them on towards the ranch. Jim said, "They stopped us so long I don't know whether we can make it into the ranch or not. We stopped too long at dinner time."

We looked back and the soldiers were very nearly out of sight. Jim said, "You other boys drive these animals. I want to see which way they go, whether they keep on a direct route. Come on, Hale." So we left the boys and started after them. We went behind some timber, and followed a long way. Soon they turned in towards the river. We then gave up following them, and rode for our men, meeting them in a couple of hours. Frank asked, "Where did they go?"

James said, "It looks funny to me. They turned in towards the river."

Lewis said, "When you mentioned the blues in the war they got on the prod."

James said, "Hale, you and Tom accept my apology, as I was so mad. I am sorry I said what I did and I hope it did not hurt your feelings. You know I like you as well as any men I ever did see. I was so mad, but I am mad at none in blue, red, or gray unless they give me a reason. We were wrong in the war, as people always are, until they leave this earth, and can be mean no more."

"Oh," I said, "Jim, we would have taken a delight to smoke the boys up some."

Tom said, "I was anxious to have them continue their sass, but Jim made them swallow all of it, and also if it had begun you would have found that old red-headed Tom would have done more to silence the boys than any of you, unless you were terribly rapid. I think I could beat Jim as he was too mad. As for hurting my feelings, you have not and can say what you wish to other people. We are friends until the last. Please mention this no more."

"Well," said I, "we had better go off our course, and turn due north, as the soldiers may turn against us, and get a lot of Mexicans and come back. They acted a little strange to me. I am of the opinion that these Mexicans are getting them to turn against us."

Jim said to Frank, "Turn them north, as we wish to mislead them if anyone should follow us. Do you suppose this last fun we have had with the Mexicans was known to the soldiers?"

"No," said Lewis, "they have not had time to get the news."

"I don't know," said Frank. "One asked what we had packed on these animals, and you know how long we were at Scott's ranch. The other girl might have told a lot when she found out that Scott and her sister were gone. I will bet that she said we characters were the boys who did it, and I believe they would give a nice lot of money to have us out of this country. If they can get these American soldiers against us it will come rocky for us. What do you think about it, Jim?"

Jim said, "Don't talk to me, as I am thinking about what has just passed." Then he rode on the side of our horses and looked as if in a deep study. It looked as though they were told about this, from their actions. Lewis said, "If we had shown weakness I believe those fellows would have wanted to see what was on those animals.

I said, "Yes, and would liked to have taken us prisoners. They are acting strangely after we have treated them so well."

"Yes," said Frank, "when a big lot dislike a fellow, all the people that have no courage or bravery stay with the largest number. We will see what Jim says later about this. We are doing well in the ranch business."

Lewis said, "It costs you all nothing to run it, from what I have learned."

I said, "It is not far off when we will stop or will have to stop at the rate we have been traveling."

Frank said, "Since James spoke about it, I would like to see the Missouri valley again."

"I would like the trip myself," Lewis said, "and hope the time will not be far off when we all will be ready to go."

Frank said, "We have had a fine time and need only handle the money and act like gentlemen." We traveled on and Tom spied a young turkey in a tree.

Tom took out his revolver and shot him dead, and tied him to his saddle, so we had turkey meat for supper and breakfast. When we had traveled about five or six miles we came across a fine lake, where the grass was fine. Jim said, "We had better camp."

So we prepared for the night, gathered wood, and cooked a fine meal. After supper we arranged our guards, and sat around and talked quite a while.

Jim said, "When we run across a buyer we had better sell and seek new fields, as they are getting too well acquainted with us here. If it is found out for certain that we did this they will offer large rewards for us, and we may have trouble with these soldiers, as they are to get money as well as us. I want you all to think this over, and we will have another talk at the ranch, as you are aware that some of these soldiers have turned against us."

Chapter 27

THESE ARE OUR LAST DAYS IN SOUTHERN TEXAS AND OLD MEXICO. WE SELL OUR PROPERTY AND GO TO MISSOURI.

Lewis was out on first guard. He was to see that none of the horses left, and that no one took us by surprise. Tom was the next guard, Frank was the next, I was the fourth, and Jim on the fifth and last. When Frank was on guard he shot a wolf, which came to steal our meat. This aroused us, and finding nothing wrong went to bed again. When we were about asleep he shot another. I got up in bed and talked to him. I asked if he had killed that one. He said no, he just broke his back like Jim did Tigo's. "Get up, and you can see him," he said. Jim said, "Frank let those wolves steal the meat. With you shooting around, anyone who wished could find us." Frank said, "I felt funny and wanted to shoot some." I said, "Frank wants me to come out and talk to him."

"Yes," said Frank, "come out and talk to me, and I will tell you a love story that happened in Missouri."

Frank went on around the horses and I got up and went on after him. We were riding and talking as usual. Frank said, "I will sit up with you and ride on your guard." He said, "When I was going to school in Missouri, before the war, I used to go and see a girl. She thought I was the real thing, and my, what a time we used to have."

"What is that yonder?" We looked, and on careful examination found it to be a large drove of wolves. The horses on that side began to get scared. We took our revolvers and killed about six of them, which aroused the others. I went in and told them the wolves were getting so thick we had to shoot them to keep them from frightening the horses. They went to bed again, and Frank said, "Let us shoot at everything." So when one got in sight we shot at him.

Jim said, "Get up, they will shoot the rest of the night. Him and Frank will not stop." So they cooked and we all ate breakfast. After breakfast, when all was ready we rode on to the ranch, and, blessed goodness, find a Scotchman and an Irishman who wanted to buy our cattle, horses, and ranch also.

The boys told us they had had some trouble with Mexicans who were trying to steal some of our cattle and horses. We learned all the news. Us four went out and had a talk whether it would be the best to leave or not. Jim says, "It will be a perfect hell if we stay here, so let us sell out and leave." This was agreed upon, and we went to the house and made a deal at once. We received for our ranch and cattle about eighty thousand dollars. We got the same men to work for the Scotch and Irish.

We stayed all night, and the next day packed our brutes and left for Galveston. I was happy to get away from such a country. We did not send a good-bye to the Mexicans at Matamoros, nor leave a lock of our hair for them. The only things we left were the noted outlaws' bodies and bones for them to remember us by.

Chapter 28

A Trip to Galveston. Me and Tom and the Smith Boys Go to Missouri. Jack Lewis Kills Two Negroes and Then Goes to Western Texas.

After a few days' drive we got to Galveston, put up our horses and mules, and sold our gold and silver for about two hundred thousand, which we divided. We began to take in Galveston. We were stopping at a hotel.

One night two negroes tried to put Lewis out of his room. Lewis told them he had paid for that room, and that it was his. They said it belonged to their rich master and he was to get out. Lewis began to talk rough to them. They said he was drunk. Lewis said, "Come and put me out." So they were mistaken for it cost them their lives. When they had reached the door Lewis took out a couple of revolvers and shot them both dead. He got his horse, and rode for the western part of Texas. We never saw Lewis again. I found out later he was killed at Las Vegas, in a fight with some Mexicans. He and Dave Pool, one of Quantrell's men, met and went to a gambling house. Dave Pool was a ranchman in Arizona. Lewis got in a dispute and the fun began. Pool was the only man that came out alive.

Us and the Smith boys came back after the Smiths were through eating and we found out what Lewis had done. There was a great stir and confusion. Their rich master offered rewards for the slayer. He was on the prod, and wanted Lewis dead or alive, for slaying his humble servants, but he was gone and they never did capture him.

After staying at this place quite awhile and disposing of our property, we boarded a steamer for New Orleans. Arriving there we put up at a hotel and had a fine old time going to balls. Tom left us one night and went walking, and four negroes tried to rob him. He killed three and wounded the other. They never found out who did this. Next day, after the shooting, Jim Smith proposed to start for Missouri, our board being paid for that night.

The Smith boys disguised and left on the next steamboat for Missouri. Me and Tom left on the one after, for we thought someone might be looking for us from Mexico. For my part I did not want any more of that country, for I was sick of such a life. Jim thought it best for us to separate. This was our last time with the Smith boys. They went to St. Louis, and from there to a county in Missouri, and settled down to a peaceable life. Jim soon married and quit his wild life and never followed it again. Frank soon after went to Colorado and was killed up there by a fellow called Hanley.

I will tell about Hanley. After shooting Frank in such a cowardly way and giving him no chance, he went to a mining camp in Colorado. He put up a gambling house and went to robbing people. At one time he swindled a fellow, who would have killed him but was prevented. This man a number of times came back to kill Hanley, but the chance never came. Hanley still kept up his robbing, and it caused the people's dislike towards him. At another time he had a fight with a man and tried to use a revolver, but the other fellow was too much for him, for he came very near beating him to death with his fist. Hanley got smitten with another gambler's girl and the two became great enemies, and quarreled often. One day he was at the table gambling, when the fellow who was mad at him put a revolver against Hanley's head and blew his brains out. So he was treated the same way as Frank. This fellow never had any trouble for killing Hanley, as it was a mining camp and had no law.

Me and Tom got on a steamer for St. Louis, and arrived about sixty hours behind the Smith boys. We did not see them for they had gone ahead.

The reason why we were late was that the steamer blew up, killing the engineer and scalding a great many more. We had to stop at a town just below where this happened. It was a great place for fun. We went to a negro church and saw them raise Cain, when they thought they were good and saved. The next night we went to a dance and danced all night, and this was another fine time. I got to talking to a girl, who seemed to enjoy my company. I was by her side most of the time. A black-headed swamp girl fell in love with Tom. Tom went so far as to ask her to marry him and she said yes, and when morning came Tom proposed to stop over and they would get married. She said her father would give her to no one, so Tom said, "Let us run away and marry."

She said, "I will go and be glad to, for my father is mean to me and whips me, and makes me do all the work."

Tom told her she would not have to work if she married him. So Tom got the license and the next morning he and the girl got on a steamer for St. Louis.

Chapter 29

TOM RILY MARRIES AND THEN I AM ALONE.

When the girl's father missed her, he made search and found her not. In a day or so he heard a man say that a fellow got a license to marry his girl. He still made inquiries and found he had lost his girl. He ripped and roared, but this did no good.

Tom was proud to go. They were a happy pair. After dinner he made inquiries for a parson, but there was none on the steamer. Tom thought of a story told of me marrying a couple at Fort Brown. I had been quiet on this but it leaked out some way. I told him I had married a couple once but my talk was too long. He said, "Long, thunder, I want you to marry us if it takes six weeks." I told him my way was a long talk and he would please excuse me. Tom said, "We will get ready while you think of the speech." So Tom and the girl got ready and called me.

I placed a book which I called for on a stool in front of them. We had quite a crowd to witness it. I told them they could take each other's right hands.

I said, "Mr. Rily will you always love and take care of this girl, and see that she never wants anything but what you will give her, if in your power?"

He said, "I will."

I now said to the girl, "Is this of your own free will and accord that you wish to marry this fellow?"

She said, "Yes."

I said, "Mr. Rily, you will have to promise me you will never love another woman as you do this one." He said he would.

I also said, "You both may kneel at the book in front of you, which you will find to be the Holy Bible, and you may take an oath to what you have said. Are you willing to do it?"

He said, "Yes."

"Now, Mr. Rily, you have made two attempts to marry and the third time you succeeded, and I will now require you to kiss the book three times and your wife once. You both may rise, and in the name of God and his servant I pronounce you man and wife."

Four or five of the people laughed for an hour. So they were married.

We went on to St. Louis. Tom and his wife stopped at the same hotel I did, and stayed there a couple of days. Then I went to seeking someone who was acquainted with father, and found a merchant who knew where he was. This man said he was in New York city. I wrote him a letter and received one in return telling me to come and see him and never go to that ranch again. The second day at the hotel Tom left, and this was the last time I ever saw him. I went to another hotel. I heard afterwards Tom became very wealthy.

After Tom and his wife left I got on a Baltimore & Southwestern train and went to New York city, and found father. He was sure glad to see me, and I him. Father had a world of money and I let him have a lot of mine, and he loaned it out on interest and it brought in a nice revenue. Father told me he was going to see a widow who had a girl about eighteen, and I could go to see her. And father wrote to the widow his son had come and that he was going to bring him down, and for her girl to have on her best rig. So me and father went down and we had a time.

I liked the girl tolerably well. She was a great talker, and of course I liked that. When me and father went home, he asked me how I liked her. I told him all right. I said, "You capture the widow and I will get the girl." Father said, "I will make the trade with you."

Next night we went to a show. Me and father were going to capture the Hampton family. Next day we went fishing. We did nothing, as we had lots of money. The girl got prettier to me and it got so I made three trips to father's one. Mrs. Hampton and father had great laughs over me and the girl's courtship.

Chapter 30

IN THE WILD WEST AGAIN. TRIP TO SOUTHWESTERN TEXAS OR SOUTHEASTERN NEW MEXICO WITH BOB DIXON.

I did nothing but talk to Grace Hampton, and we certainly loved one another. We went to a show one night, and it was fine. One saying I remember quite well. One fellow was telling a lot of funny jokes to some girls, and asked, "Did you ever hear of the story of the empty jug?"

They said, "No, tell us."

"Yes, I will tell you there was nothing in it."

The next was some negro minstrels and a white man. The negro told of a terrible accident, which occurred in the settlement. It was about an old mule who done so much work in the settlement. The people had died, and he was in trouble over it. The white fellow said he would sing and play some for him. So he began to play and sing, and the negro began to cry. The white man stopped and the negro did the same. Then he commenced to play again, and the negro began to cry. The white man said, "I was playing and singing so everything would not be so gloomy to you, and when I play and sing you cry."

"Well," said the negro, "I can not keep from it, for your voice is so much like that old mule braying, and I cannot keep from crying."

The next negro said his girl gave a play party. One play he would always remember, and that was "Heavy hangs over your head," his girl's father hung a chair over his head. The other jokes I will not repeat.

After the show was over me and the girl went home. My, my, the way I was liking this girl was a shame. I made a proposal to this girl, that me and her have one name instead of two. She told me she never did see anyone she liked half as well as me, and said when she went to school two more years she would marry me. I told her this would seem like two hundred years to me.

Father and mother went on another pleasure trip to Baltimore. Us children went along also, and we had another fine trip. Me and Grace would walk around and look at the town, and when we got tired of walking, we would take boat rides. Time soon passed pleasantly and very soon we boarded a train for New York. I was in love with this girl, and asked if she would not make the time shorter. She said she could not as her mother would not allow it. She said she loved me but her mother would make her go to school that long anyway. So the school began. She was away most of the time, and the days were lonely after she went to school.

One day I ran on Bob Dixon. He said in a couple of days he was going to his ranch, and said, "I want you to go with me, and stay awhile if not all the time." So I studied over the subject a great deal, and concluded to go. I told father about my bad luck, and about his step-daughter not wanting to marry for a couple of years, and that her mother wished her to go to school that long.

"Yes," said father, "you will have to wait." I then told him I was going with Bob Dixon to his ranch in southwestern Texas.

He said, "You are having a fine time here and had better stay."

I said, "No, I am going, I want to see the Wild West again." So I got everything ready. It took me quite a while to tell my girl good-bye. She cried, and I told her I loved her better than anyone I ever saw and when two years were up, I would be back to get her. She said she was afraid I never would come back, and that the Mexicans or Indians might kill me. I kissed her good-bye and she went on to school.

I went with my grip to where Dixon was, and that day boarded a train for St. Louis. After staying there two or three days we went on to Kansas City, and stopped there one day to look over the town. We found very little at this place. It was almost as rough as the Rocky Mountains. In fact I never saw such a rough place selected for a town.

Me and Dixon, after looking over Kansas City, got on an Atchison and Topeka train for New Mexico. After a long run we came to a station in Colorado, by the name of La Hunta or La Junta.

We stopped at this place one day and night, and went to a Mormon ball, given by some Mormons. We danced by numbers, and the man who called the numbers would not call Dixon's number when he came to it. The next time he came around he called his own name instead of Dixon's, and Bob was going to eat him up alive if he did not call the name right. The Mormon ikes began to crowd in and I said, "Dixon, stomp him through the floor, and I will kill everyone that tries to get to you." So the Mormon laid down his colors, after Dixon spit in his face and rubbed it around like a shoe black trying to shine a shoe. Then the lads showed weakness. From that on everything went as nicely as possible. And what a time me and Dixon had when not on the floor. We were in the corner with a Mormon miss telling it scary to her. And I don't believe there was anyone that had any better time than we two. The Mormon boys and men did not like to see me and Dixon have such a nice time and be so

gauly, but there was no way for them to help themselves, but declare war and raise their flag. The
first pass Dixon made was enough for them.

In the later part of the night me and Dixon left
and went to bed, to get some sleep, before the
Santa Fe came, going south. The Santa Fe train
was late and never came until ten next day. So
when she did get in we crawled on her, bound for
Las Vegas, New Mexico, getting there about dark.
We put up at a hotel, and after supper went prowling around town. We had plenty to drink, for you
could get anything you wanted. At the dry goods
and grocery houses they had all kinds of drinks
free.

There were two sides to this town – Mexican
part and the white part. Me and Dixon were
amused at the people here. After staying here four
or five days, we got in a hack and went to a Mexican town, named Anton Chico.

We had not been there long until about twenty
Bar Z boys came in and shot the town up and ran
most of the Mexicans out. The Bar Z was a cattle
brand, and their ranch was close to this town. What
men they had were Americans and the people said
it was a common thing for them to shoot the gambling houses full of holes. It was funny to me and
Dixon to see them shoot around in town.

Me and Dixon stayed one day and then got in a hack for Fort Sumner. So we drove to Sumner, which was a Mexican town. We stayed all night at this place, and the next day we drove for Roswell. This place is located in the Pecos Valley. We stayed at Roswell two or three days. It is a pretty place, small streams or rivers not over five miles away. Dixon, on account of sheep coming in his range, was forced to move close to Seven Rivers, in Lincoln county, New Mexico.

We branded calves all that summer and that fall Dixon sent two herds to southern Kansas, close to Liberal. Sam Urs had charge of the herd in front and I the one behind. We got along fine until we got east of Fort Sumner. It began to rain and the cattle drifted badly, and left their bed ground. We stayed with them and managed to hold them, but were quite a ways from camp next morning when daylight came. When we did get back some of our horses were gone. We did not move our camp very far, and that day found all but seven of our horses. Next morning I sent Jim Henry to find them. He soon ran across them and soon overtook us.

We traveled along until we reached the Canadian river a little above the Texas line, and coming to this found the water too high to cross. We had to stop there a couple of days to let the waters get lower, and then came very near not getting our cattle across, but we managed to make them ford it, and moved a piece north to camp. Urs was getting a big start on us, and was a long way ahead. We moved along nicely, but had some trouble to keep our horses. Next day we met a lot of Indians on their way to the Panhandle hunting buffalo. They said they were scarce, and were going to where there were heap buffaloes. They jabbered and talked quite awhile, until we rode on and left them and they went their way. We arrived at the ranch all right and delivered, and started back.

We stopped at a town in the Panhandle of Texas by the name of Tascosa, and took in a ball that night. Tascosa was a Mexican town, and they gave a ball and we all went. Some of my men got to drinking, and we had to lay them out until they got so they could go to camp and to bed. A fellow by the name of Henry got to paying too much attention to a señorita, and the Mexican lover of hers got jealous. The Mexicans are easily offended. The girl liked Henry and was glad to talk to him, and the Mexican who brought her there got mad and made a talk and said what he was going to do for Henry. Henry kept on talking to his girl and took her to a lunch, so the boys said. I was not there at that time. The latter part of the night he said he was going to kill gringo, and started back at him with a knife. Henry out with a revolver and was going to kill him, but some of the boys kept him from doing so. The women left after this and the boys shot the house full of holes, and then came to camp and went to bed.

The next day we went to a creek called the Alamocitas, and after the wagons started from the camp the boys went by the ballroom and filled it with lead again. We traveled along all right until we got to Fort Sumner. We stayed at this place one night, and we heard that another ball was in progress, so we all turned out. We got along fine with our dancing until about twelve at night. A Mexican damsel would not dance with Tom Mills, so he became mad and came out with a couple of revolvers and began to shoot in the roof of the building, and the Mexicans ran over one another trying to get out. So the Fort Sumner ball was ended, and we all went to the camp and went to bed.

Next morning we harnessed up our chuck teams and went down the Rio Pecos, which means river Pecos. When we got ready to go, Henry and the boys went by and shot the houses full of holes. Urs' men came up and they wasted a lot of ammunition also. After they raised Cain for quite awhile, and though everyone had seen them, they rode down the Rio Pecos, after the wagons and horses, and in about four days we reached Roswell and had a great fish fry on the river Hondo and Spring river. Anyone could catch fish in these streams as fast as he wished.

From there we went on to the ranch and gave up our horses and men. There were three letters there for me – from father, Grace, and her mother. Father told me that Grace was as pretty as ever, and wanted me to come back, and spoke often about me. Grace wrote if I ever came to that country again she would never let me leave, for she said it was so lonely not seeing me, and I must think of those two years she spoke of. Her mother said they were all lost by me being gone, and a whole lot more I will not repeat. This made me think of home and I wanted to go back.

After we had been back a day or so, some of the Mexicans from the White Mountains stole some of Dixon's horses and tried to get away with them. Me and eight of our men went in pursuit, Henry, Simpson, Mills, Anders, and some more. We followed the Mexicans three days, and at the end of the third day we met a Mexican boy who told us where they were camped, and also that they had a lot of horses they had purchased in Lincoln county. We ran on some of the horses and they were Dixon's. We came on the camp and charged and the Mexicans went to the brush. We burned everything in the camp, and took all the horses, and started for the

Seven Rivers ranch. We drove all night the first night, and rested next day; but we had a guard out during the day for fear of surprise. We at last reached the ranch, and turned our horses loose. After staying there a day or so me and Dixon went on a pleasure trip to Lincoln, county seat of Lincoln county.

Chapter 31

WAR IN LINCOLN COUNTY, NEW MEXICO, KNOWN AS THE LINCOLN COUNTY WAR.

Me and Dixon got to Lincoln all O.K., and put up at a small boarding house. Lincoln was a one-horse place, and I will not describe it. It would not take but a few words. We stayed in Lincoln several days. It was a tough place – out-laws, etc., but was too dull for me and Dixon, so we went to Fort Sumner and stayed there the rest of the winter.

Me and Dixon got to be great friends with a big ranchman by the name of Chisholm and stayed part of our time with him. There was lots of fighting and killing around Sumner. There was a young fellow from Lincoln county that came to this part, and he was a great outlaw and had killed three of Chisholm's men.

This young fellow's nickname was Billy the Kid. Cowmen call boys kids. The reason this kid made so many trips to Fort Sumner was because he was smitten on a part Mexican and English girl and came to see her often. The Mexican's name for part

English and part American is Coyote. The kid came to see this girl once, and when he got back to the ranch he found his great friend murdered. He was owner of a ranch, and was a young Englishmen.

I will give a few words about Billy the Kid. It is necessary, as we fought against one another during the Lincoln County War. The kid, so I heard, was born in New York, and at the age of seventeen his parents moved to Silver City, New Mexico, and put up a boarding house. After staying there awhile, the kid shot and killed a negro soldier in self-defense. The next man he killed was a blacksmith, and not according to law. He left Silver City and went to the western part of Arizona, where he soon learned to be perfect with cards. After staying in Arizona awhile he went to Old Mexico and began to work for a cattleman, in the state of Chihuahua.

One night he and the cowboys went in town and commenced gambling. The kid went to gambling with a rich Mexican, playing monte. The Mexican and the kid got in a dispute and the kid drew a revolver and shot him full of holes. From here he went to Texas, and later on went to Lincoln county, New Mexico, and began to work for a young Englishman by the name of Tunsal. This Englishman and the kid were great friends. After the kid came in from Fort Sumner and heard of Tunsal being killed by a lot of men from the Rio Pecos he swore he would kill everyone. The kid killed them before the stockmen's or cattlemen's war ended.

A great many other things caused this war, which I will tell you very little about. Still, I am writing on the subject. After the kid came in and his great friend, the Englishman, was dead, he and a lot more started in pursuit. But Norton and his men made their escape. This started the Lincoln County War. In the spring Dixon's outfit took sides with Chisholm's gang against the kid. There were many stockmen and their men in the war. So it was equally divided. We would have been in very little of this, but we had moved up close to the Y ranch. So this involved us. The kid killed two of the men who murdered Tunsal, and then rode to Lincoln. He was corralled in a building by some of our own men. They set fire to the building, which was surrounded by a lot of soldiers and some Seven River Indians, also our men. The reason us and Dixon did not like the kid was because he had murdered the sheriff of Don Ana county. While the building was burning the kid played on a piano all the while. He said he did that to entertain the crowd on the outside. When the house was all afire the kid and his crowd came out facing lead and fire. Everybody was killed but Tom Ophollard [O'Folliard] and the kid. They seemed to have charmed lives. The war ended that fall, and many a cowboy and ranchman was placed under the sod. The kid killed every man that murdered his friend.

After the war was over the kid stole a lot of horses from the Seven River Indians, who they had just gotten through fighting. Some called them the Seven River warriors, who drove them across the plains, or the Panhandle of Texas, to a Mexican town by the name of Tascosa. At this place they sold them for a nice lot of money. The Seven River Indians followed them quite a ways and gave up the chase. The Seven River warriors hated the kid, for he had killed so many of their men during this cattlemen's war. The kid and his men stayed at Tascosa a long time spending their wealth on cards and whiskey.

Chapter 32

THE KID RETURNS FROM THE TEXAS PANHANDLE AND KILLS A MAN AT FORT SUMNER, AND SHOOTS ONE OF HIS OWN MEN THROUGH THE SHOULDER.

After the kid and his men had spent most of their money, they came back to New Mexico, to continue their outlaw work. After getting back to Fort Sumner he had to kill a man, to give anyone an idea how rapid he was with a revolver.

I will tell about this killing. After the kid and his men came back from Tascosa, they spent their idle time around Sumner. They had a great many enemies at this place, caused by the war, and, as I was going to say, the kid was leaning against the wall of the house, when a man said to another, "I will bet the drinks I can kill a man before you can." The other fellow said, "I will take the bet." The first man out with his revolver and snapped it twice at the kid. The kid out with his revolver and shot him six times before he touched the floor. He began to fall at the first shot.

After the kid killed his man he out with a couple of revolvers and said, "All you fist and bantams walk up, and have something to drink, or I will shoot some more." So they walked up and took the medicine, thinking it best. The kid still stayed around here. He was going to see a rich fellow's half-sister. The man's name was Maxwell. Her given name I have forgotten.

After staying here awhile, the kid went down the Pecos Valley and stole some more horses. He also took some of ours, and took them somewhere in the Panhandle and sold them. While in the Panhandle of Texas he stole a lot of cattle from those stockmen and drove them to the Capitan Mountains in New Mexico, and sold them to a man by the name of Coglin. Coglin then drove them to the White Mountains, and then came around White Oaks to hide. I had just come from Seven Rivers, when a man came from White Oaks wanting help from our ranch to capture the kid. Me and Dixon had a talk and concluded to send some men. I got in the notion to go along, so we started out, and getting to the Oaks, found a crowd ready to go. They were under Jim Caralyle [Carlyle].

While hunting out the hills we came on the kid and one of his men cooking breakfast. Seeing us they fired a shot apiece and ran to the mountains, leaving their saddles, horses, and breakfast. We knew they could not hide their tracks and we went back to White Oaks after something to eat and more men. On getting more men we came back and started on the trail. A few miles brought us to the Great House ranch. We circled around to make sure and found no trails leading out, and we thought they were ours and made breastworks of logs, etc., and waited for daylight to come. The snow was deep, and had been on the ground several days, and it was cold and disagreeable to be out. After so long a time, daylight began to appear, which we were anxious to see.

Chapter 33

THE KID KILLS JIM CARALYLE AND MAKES HIS ESCAPE TO ANTONCHICO AND STEALS SOME HORSES.

Towards sunup Jim Great House sent a negro to get the horses, and the negro had not gotten very far before he was captured by us, and on asking questions we found out the kid and six of his men were stopping with them. We said we would storm the house and take them. Some objected and said, give them a chance for their lives. We sent back the negro with a note, telling them they were surrounded, and if they would come out and surrender, they would be treated as prisoners. If not, they would have to stand an assault, and be swung up to a tree. The kid wrote back an insulting note, saying, "You fellows go to the hot place, or somewhere else." Some of us wanted to charge and take them dead or alive, and some said give them a chance for their lives. So we sent Mr. negro with another note, saying we would send no more, that they should come out with their hands up.

A new messenger came out. It was Jim Great House, proprietor of the ranch, saying the kid wished a talk with our leader. The Oak boys asked who would insure that the leader would not be hurt. Great house said he would vouch for it, and if Caralyle gets hurt they could do the same to him, and says, "I am willing to take an oath the kid will not hurt him. He has nothing against Caralyle." So James Caralyle went to have a talk with the kid, but never returned to us alive. After Caralyle had gotten in the house he and the kid talked about a great many things, and the kid ordered up the drinks, and told Jim to come up and drink to his health. Jim did not like to do this, but had to because he was under their command.

After they drank the whiskey and Wilson had taken in the glasses, the kid saw a glove in Jim's pocket. "Jim, was you with those men yesterday who caused me to walk through that snow?...." "Yes," replied Jim. It made the kid mad, as the snow was knee deep and it was very wearisome. "Well, Jim, walk up and take your last drink on this earth, for I am going to kill you." Wilson was the one who gave the drinks. After drinking the kid told Jim to kneel, and say his prayers. Then the kid took aim and fired, but not at Jim. "Well," said the kid, "you are not dead yet. Come, let us take another drink. Jim, did you think I would shoot you that way and give you no chance? Rush around Wilson, and give us something to drink, for I am satisfied Jim is dry." So Wilson handed out the drinks.

The shot on the inside made us think it meant Caralyle's death. A man wrote a note and sent it back by the negro, and the note sent back read thus: "If Caralyle is not out here in ten minutes, your friend Great House will be shot."

The kid read this note so Caralyle could hear it, and wrote back: "Caralyle is safe. I am not through with him yet, and if I hear a shot on the outside I will think you have killed Great House, and then I will pay you back by killing Caralyle."

All of this was read to Caralyle. The negro had no more than got to us with the note, when another man behind another breastworks shot at the house to make some noise, not knowing the threats. Jim, hearing the shot, jumped through the window. The kid shot him several times before he touched the ground. He died in view of his friends. Great House gave his guards the slip, and went to the mountains like a deer. We shot at the house until late, but did no damage. We went back to the Oaks to get something to eat and more men, and then were going to come back and capture the kid and he would never know we had been gone. About twelve that night the kid and his men headed north with firearms in hand and were going to fight their way out, but to their happiness they found no one.

We returned before daylight and found they had gotten away, but we followed after them until we came to the Spencer ranch. This ranch was owned by a man who informed us that the kid and his men had eaten breakfast with him about an hour before and had gone on their way. We followed the trail about an hour until we came to a rough country, where we would have to take it on foot. We went back and were going to hang the old man, but some objected.

We then went to the Great House ranch and burned houses, sheds, and everything. The kid and his men walked into Antonchico, and there stole a horse apiece and supplied themselves with money. They then rode down the Rio Pecos to Fort Sumner. We went back to White Oaks, staying there a couple of days, after which we Dixon men went back to the ranch. Up above Salt creek, we told them of our bad luck in gaining nothing, and about Caralyle being killed. Caralyle was a fine man. Dixon says this young man has killed so many this way, but we may get to capture him yet.

Everything was getting along all right. Jim Daylor, who was working for Dixon, killed about three Mexicans; he was courting a señorita. This girl's father and mother lived on a creek that emptied in the Salt creek, and Daylor got her smitten on him and went to see her often and had things his own way. There was a young Mexican who also loved her. Because she liked Daylor better he became mad and planned with his Mexican friends to dispose of Daylor. What leisure time Daylor had, he put in going to see this girl. They would talk or walk around or go horseback riding in the hills. This put the young Mexican in a rage. Daylor stayed there two days courting this girl, and one time while starting for home three Mexicans met him and tried to kill him. After he had emptied three revolvers there were three Mexicans and two horses dead. So Daylor rushed to the ranch and told Dixon what he had done. Dixon advised him to leave. He got well prepared with firearms.

He then started for the Panhandle of Texas via the way of Fort Sumner. He had been gone only about thirty-six hours before a gang of Mexicans came, wanting to capture and kill him. They asked where he was and we told them he had been gone several days. They talked a lot and got sassy. We came out with a lot of guns and told them to go, and they went in a hurry and we never saw them any more.

Chapter 34

THE CAPTURE OF BILLY THE KID AND HIS MEN AT STINKING SPRINGS.

We had been at the ranch only a few days when Barney Mason came and wanted us to help capture the kid, who was around the Fort Sumner country. Mason at one time was one of the kid's men. After the last horse raid the kid and Mason got in a dispute, and the kid out with a Winchester and shot him through the shoulder and Mason fell. The kid thought he had killed him but he had not. Mason was here to get help.

Dixon said all could go who wanted, so me and five others went. Getting to Fort Sumner a small crowd was there with the sheriff, Pat Garret [Garrett]. Two of Sirrango's [Siringo] men were there and the manager of the LX Company had sent two of his men to help capture the kid. We numbered about fourteen.

After getting to Sumner it began to snow and kept up for about four days and nights until the ground was covered to great depth. We put in some of our time around the fires until some of the snow had melted. The spy reported that the kid and his men would be in from Portales that night, so the sheriff got a building on the Portales road and put out a guard to watch and tell us. We put in our time around the fires playing seven-up, poker, and monte. All at once the guard threw open the door and says "Garret, there comes a crowd down the road." We all ran out with our guns in our hands and hid behind a wall. When they got close Garret says, "Throw up your hands." He had no more than said the word than we fired. They went away except one and that was the kid's favorite man whose name was Tom Ophollard. He had several bullet holes through his body.

We followed the trail until we came to a small house. They had their horses tied in front. We got down and went up to the building. Garret and Hall went close to the door to watch it. We built fires and took turns relieving one another. About daylight one of the kid's men came to the door, but a couple of shots from Garret's and Hall's guns sent him over the way. This aroused the others who thought of escape. The kid had his horse on the inside and says, "If we can get the others in we will rush out and try to get away." And when they had gotten the first animal partly in, we shot it dead. This blocked the way so the boys had to give this up also and surrendered.

Next day the kid was taken towards Lincoln, and from there was taken to Don Ana and tried before Judge Bristol for the murder of the sheriff during the Lincoln County War, and was sentenced to be hanged in April. He was turned over to Pat Garret to see that it was done. Garret took him back and put him in prison until the said day. There being no prison at that time, Garret used his office or a room above, and had the kid handcuffed and shackled and also two guards to watch him. He told the guard to watch him close and if he tried to get away, kill him. I will now skip some before I mention the kid's name again.

Chapter 35

A Trip Back to the Ranch, and Then Go to the Black Hills in Dakota with a Steer Herd.

After we captured the kid we put in our time around the ranch drifting back cattle that had scattered during the snow storms. After the first of March Dixon came in from Las Vegas, and said he was going to have three thousand steers driven to the Black Hills in Dakota, and would like me to take charge of this herd as I understood driving herds. I told him I had just as soon go to the Black Hills as Old Mexico, in fact, had rather.

We had lots of corn horses and began work on the eighth day of March, and was soon ready to go to the hills where Lynch's ranch was. Lynch was the man Dixon sold these steers to. We started and the first day's travel was nice. The steers did not want to be held under herd as they did not want to leave their old range. They were very poor and during the coming night we had some trouble to hold them. In a day or so the Mexican horse rustler had a fight with our negro cook, and the cook came very near killing him. At first the cook was getting the best of it. The Mexican got his knife to shorten the work, but the cook's spade was handy so he knocked the Mexican down with it and beat him. The only thing which kept him from killing the Mexican was one of the cowboys rode up and put a stop to it. The Mexican was very near killed and was difficult to arouse. He was left at a Mexican's house to receive medical attention, which we were not able to give. We at last reached the Rio Pecos and crossed it, and camped to the right of the avenue close to the trees, opposite the fort. Two of my men went to town to have some fun, and got to playing cards. The Mexican monte dealer won all their money, so they said it will never do to leave town without money. The boys were drinking too much, so they went back and put a revolver in his face. Some of the others put all the money on the gambling table in their pockets, and ordered him out to their horses and relieved him of his revolver. Telling him good-bye they rode a roundabout way, to where the wagon was camped, yelling, for they felt their whiskey. They woke me up and told me they had had bad luck in gambling, but had fine luck in taking.

I employed another Mexican to look after our horses and mules. Next morning we left the camp ground and moved a little east and camped close to the Horseshoe ranch. Next day went close to the Coviawa, which means horse. We were getting along fine with our herd. We had to go slow on account of them being so poor. That night we camped and the next day we went close to the Coonavar.

The next day the Mexican and negro cook had a little trouble. It seemed as though the negro had a habit of working Mexicans over. The negro was baking bread and cooking meat, when the Mexican became hungry, and went in the oven where the bread was baking. The negro carried his shovel to the chuck box, after he had put some coals of fire on his oven, and looking around saw the greaser in the bread, helping himself. So he grabbed up the spade and threw it at the Mexican, hitting him on the side of the head and knocking him senseless. I was riding up and saw it. The negro pulled him out of the way and went on cooking.

I asked the negro why he did it. He said "Massa, white man can go in my cooking, but a black man like him cannot. I will learn these Mexicans something if they monkey with this negro, and they can't act like white people before this child. They have to stand around."

I got some water and put in the Mexican's face and brought him to life again. I then sent him to his horses and told him never to touch anything the cook had. He said he would not. We went on without any more trouble with our men. We were traveling very slow and reached the Canadian river. The water was high on account of the snow melting in the mountains. We stayed a few days at the Canadian waiting for the waters to get lower. Later on we swam our cattle and horses over, but the chuck wagon could not go, so we were in a bad condition. The negro cook made a boat out of a log and when he cooked he would bring us something to eat. He also brought our beds so we would have something to sleep on while not on guard. In a day or so we managed to get our wagon across, and I felt a great deal better than when it was on the other side.

Chapter 36

THE NEGRO COOK SHOOTS THE MEXICAN HORSE RUSTLER. THE MEXICAN THOUGHT HE WOULD USE HIS SPADE AGAIN, BUT WAS MISTAKEN.

After getting our wagon across the Canadian river we made a drive northward, as the grass was not very good on the Canadian. After the first day's travel from the river, I went ahead to camp the wagon for dinner. I took the horses with me to give them time to graze, before the herd came up. I camped the wagon where I wanted the cook to get dinner. I told the Mexican to get wood, and I went back to the herd to see how it was getting along. After I was gone the Mexican got the wood for the cook and ran at the cook with a knife. The cook out with his revolver and shot him twice with his only ammunition. I suppose twice, by the blood that was around and from what the negro said. The Mexican ran and got on his horse and left. That was the last we ever saw of the Mexican.

Mason went out to see if he had died, but found nothing. He said the greaser kept in a straight line, and was satisfied he had a place selected to go. His money due him was not worth the horse. Just the same I was glad he was gone.

We moved after dinner about five or six miles and camped for the night. I don't think the negro slept any, thinking the Mexican would come back. We traveled on and came to the Beaver creek, a prong of the Canadian river. After getting in the territory one of the boys roped a buffalo, and, not having his revolver with him, thought he would tie it down and cut its throat, but failed. His horse was not good to rope and hold on and every time the buffalo wanted to it hooked his horse, so he gave it up. He threw down his rope, one end of which was around the animal's neck, and let it go. He came in camp and told of his bad luck. We wished he had killed the buffalo, as the meat would have been nice. Buffalo were getting scarce in the United States now.

We traveled on and towards night began to look like a rain storm was due. We camped before night and gathered plenty of wood, so we could have a fine fire and keep the camp located, if it got very dark. We caught our horses and relieved the other boys, who were on day herd. We could hear the distant thunder in the west, which told us that a storm cloud was approaching. So we began to make preparations for the coming night. We put much wood together, and when night did come we set it on fire. As soon as it began to get dark, the rain began to fall and it was cold and disagreeable. The cattle began to drift badly and were hard to keep together. One of the boy's horses got his foot in a dog hole and fell, and scared the cattle pretty badly. He caught his horse without any trouble. The rain fell until near daylight and then it ceased. I then went in and woke up the other boys, and they relieved us who had been up all night. I then aroused the cook, who put the coffee pot on the fire and began to cook breakfast. We lost but a few cattle and they were not far off next morning. We had no trouble in putting them in the herd.

After we had all changed horses, we moved out a couple of miles, and us who had been up all night went to bed and got some sleep, which we needed badly. The clouds had disappeared by dinner time, and the weather was fair. We went on guard and had a pretty night of it. The grass began to grow and our cattle began to improve in looks. It was a great help to our horses. We traveled on until we reached the Arkansas river. I should have told in a day's travel we met a government outfit, which came up and stopped close to us for dinner. They were on their way to Kiowa, Kansas, and were from Colorado Springs. There was a young man with them who wanted to work for me. I gave him employment and put him with the horses, for he would have been no good with the cattle, having no experience, and would have been a perfect nuisance. He left the government band and came over to us, and I mounted him.

Chapter 37

THE COLORADO BOY ROPES A BEAR. HIS HORSE BUCKS HIM OFF, AND THE SADDLE COMES OFF AND IS LEFT WITH THE BEAR, WHO CHEWS SOME OF THE RIGGING OFF.

The government band went on after dinner and we began to shove our cattle together for the drive to the Arkansas river. Tom Allen told the Colorado boy about one of the boys roping a buffalo and his horse not being good to rope on, he could do nothing with it. I put Allen there as the rustler was a beginner. The rustler asked Allen if his horses were good to rope on. Allen said, "They cannot be beaten." Allen told something that was not so, for very few of rustler's horses are good to rope on, as the work does not require good horses.

After Allen told the boy about the buffalo he was anxious to rope something on his pack saddle, and he got a chance next day on the Arkansas river. We camped that evening.

Bright and early next morning we were driving for the Arkansas, getting there at eleven-thirty, and camped for dinner.

Our Colorado horse rustler saw a bear and thought he would rope him and bring him to camp. Prowling around close, he threw his rope at the bear, which went around his neck. His horse got scared and threw him off, and ran away. The weight of the bear pulled the saddle off and it jumped on the saddle and began to chew the leather, very little of which was on it. It was no fine saddle like ours. While the bear was on his saddle, he ran to camp and told us how a bear had gotten in his rope, and caused his horse to buck him off. Mills got on my horse, which was still saddled, and went up there. He found the saddle, but no rope. The bear had made his escape. Allen laughed about the rustler doing this and getting in trouble. Allen had been thrown off just the same, and I laughed.

We crossed the Arkansas and moved about four miles and camped for the night. The Colorado boy patched up his saddle, for it was torn up some. He said he was going to rope no more, as he did not think his horses good rope horses, and did not believe they were gentle. Next morning we got to moving early, and Allen was on day herd. He found a rusty-headed badger and put his rope around him, and commenced playing with him.

The badger was very poor and could not run fast. Allen got to pulling him up to the horse's nose. The horse was afraid of the badger, which would stand on his hind feet and squeal. The badger got mad and fastened his teeth in the horse's nose, and made him pitch. Allen was a fine broncho rider, but the horse threw him and ran away, so Allen came in camp on foot. The Colorado boy, when Alien came in this way, thought it so funny he yelled. Allen got my horse and caught his. After his horse left him it ran back to the other horses. I laughed about this often. The rustler said he was well pleased over it.

A Mexican came up after dinner and wanted work, but I was afraid to employ him, as the negro was such a fine cook that I did not want him to leave. He told some of the boys that if a Mexican did get work again he was going to leave. So the Mexicans had all been failures, and I would not hire him.

We traveled on and camped for the night. The next morning we discovered some of our horses were gone, so we had to stop a day to look them up. First half day we could not find them, but some of the boys went out after dinner, and towards night, Will Hickman brought them in. He had found them close to the Arkansas river, feeding nicely on the grass. Towards night a drove of men came and camped a mile from us. They had a drove of mustangs, or wild horses, they had caught in the hills and on the plains.

Chapter 38

I Employ a Young Negro, Who Drives the Horses in the Day Time and the Colorado Lad Herds Them at Night. The Negro Horse Rustler Gets Drunk at Pueblo, Colorado, and Tries to Whip the Negro Cook, Who Whips Him Mighty Near to Death with a Mule Whip.

The man who owned the horses and wagons came over to see us and made inquiries where we were going. I told him we were driving a herd to the Black Hills to a ranchman by the name of Lynch. That we were representing a fellow who lived in the Pecos Valley of New Mexico, by the name of Dixon. I asked him where he was going. He said to Medicine Lodge, Kansas, to sell the horses he had captured. He said when he sold this bunch he was going to quit the business and go to St. Louis. He also asked me if I wanted to employ a negro. I told him, if reliable. He said he had one who wanted to work for a cattleman and was a fine workman. He was about eighteen and had a saddle and two horses. I told him to tell the negro to come over. So he got on his horse and went to his men. Pretty soon came the negro, riding a horse and leading another with a bed on his back, and asked if this was the wagon and men who wished to give a darkey work. I told him to get down and turn his horses loose and prepare his bed, that I would start him to work next morning.

He was up and helped the other negro cook to get breakfast. After breakfast I told him he could go along with the horses and drive them, and be a horse rustler, and get them up when we would need them. He and the other negro got to loving one another, and became as thick as thieves. A little later they were not quite so loving. I will tell you about their fight later. The new negro proved to be a fine worker and attended to what you told him.

Next morning we moved camp as usual. Everything went nicely and in a few days we camped close to Pueblo, Colorado. At this place we stopped one day, and all but five, who were watching the day herd, went to town. The negro horse rustler wanted to go, and as one of the boys said he did not care about going, that he would watch the horses for him, the negro went to town with us. The last I saw of him he was buying some clothes, so me and the other boys went prowling around town.

About ten we went back to the camp and met the fellow who stayed to watch the horses for the negro. He was smiling, so I said, "What is the matter with you?"

He said, "The two negroes had a fight. Not much of a fight, either."

I said, "Tell us about it."

"I suppose after the negro went to town and bought his clothes he bought some whiskey also. Then he came to camp on a run, and told the cook he wanted to whip someone, and called him some names. The cook was cutting beef for dinner. The cook said, 'You better quit calling me names. White man can call me names but a black negro or Mexican cannot.' I was lying on a bed looking at them. The other negro said, 'I will call you what I want to, and whip you besides.' So he ran after our cook with a rope and hit him with it. The first thing the cook did was to knock him down, then getting his mule whip he got on his head and began to beat him until he began to yell. The cook whipped him until he sobered up. It looked like the cook was going to finish him up. I went and jerked the cook off him, and the other negro went and lay down on the grass, for he was hurt pretty badly. The cook went on with his work."

After he got through telling us we rode on into camp, and saw the negro, who had gotten the worst of the fight, up against a bed, which was rolled up. I told him to go and get the other horses, for we wanted to change after dinner and relieve the other boys. He ran to his horse and rushed around in a hurry, and soon brought up the horses. He and the other negro were not as good friends as before.

After dinner I had the boys catch fresh horses and relieve those on day herd. After dinner the boys who had been on day herd went to take it in, and got to drinking and got three sheets in the wind. We then moved northward, and in a few days came to Colorado Springs. This place was known as a great health resort. The prettiest of all was Pike's Peak. One day a small rain cloud came up, or between us and the peak, and we could see the top of the peak above the cloud. I could tell the height of this peak, but have forgotten.

This was a great country for game, as deer, wolves, and a great many other animals. Me and Allen went hunting and killed four deer and one large wolf. That coming night there came up a thunder storm. It rained hardly a drop and had thunder and lightning only. Thunder storms like this I was not anxious to be in again.

We traveled on until we came close to Denver. Our cattle were getting fat, for the grass was fine.

I sent one of the boys to Denver to see if there was any mail for us. He returned by dinner time.

He had four letters for me. One was from Dixon, telling me that Billy, the Kid, had made his escape after killing his two guards, and was making his home in the Fort Sumner district. The next letter was from Lynch, in the Black Hills. He wanted to know how I was getting along with the herd, and said I should write to him, which I did. I wrote and told him where we were, that there was such an improvement in the steers' looks since we had left the Pecos Valley he would not recognize them.

The other letter was from father, in New York. He was wanting me to come home, and said he was now about sixty years old and was getting feeble. He said, "I have plenty of money, so come home, and what money you have and what I will give you, will be plenty for you to live at ease. So come by fall. I hope you are tired of ranch life now. Grace wants to see you so bad."

As soon as I read this I swore I would go as soon as I reached Lynch's ranch, but I did not. I went all the way back to Dixon's ranch on the Rio Pecos, and then went back that fall.

Chapter 39

A LETTER FROM MY GIRL. I WANT TO LEAVE THE WILD WEST.

The fourth letter was from my girl at New York city. She said she had been lost and very lonely since I had left. And, "You said you were too old for me, that I would find someone else I would like better. I have not and never will. Come back this fall and we will marry, if you want me, or like me. Your father wants you to come home. And please come. Signed Grace."

I became a little excited and said, "I am going to do that."

Enson said, "What is that you are going to do?"

I said, "I am going to see my girl."

One of the boys said, "If you go to that country you will marry some of those girls, and we will never see you again."

"Well," said I, "there is always one to fill the place of another, so someone can fill my place in this western country. And if my position cannot be filled there will be someone wanting."

We traveled on with our cattle, and had some rainy weather. We soon reached the South Platte river, and the waters were too deep to cross on account of so much rain. We stayed here three days, and after the water got lower we crossed, and went a day's travel north of it. That night our horses became scared and ran away from the night watchman, the Colorado boy. I think the cougars scared them, as the next day we found one killed and almost eaten up, and tracks about eight inches in diameter. We were satisfied they did it, as cougars love horse meat. It took all day to find all our horses. The coming night we put three men to guard them, and had them fire off a revolver to keep the cougars off. Next morning we were on the road early. Hinton shot and killed a cougar next morning. I suppose it had been watching our horses, but was afraid to come very close.

We traveled on north. The cattle were getting pretty, as they were getting so fat. The time passed slowly since I heard from home, and I thought of all the past. I knew the time would be short, yet it would seem very long. We still drifted on northward, and soon reached Cheyenne, Wyoming. Some of the boys went to town and had a fine time.

Me and one of the others stayed around camp and killed a beef, as we were running low on meat. And in the evening a panther wanted to come in camp after some fresh meat. I presume it had had bad luck and could catch nothing. I got my Winchester and shot him. He gave some screams and fell on his side, dead. He was a large one, and, by his looks, seemed to be an old one, for his teeth were badly worn, and claws broken. We stayed here all night. The boys came in from town, but did not bring any mail. We then caught night horses and prepared for the night.

After supper the boys told those on day herd to come in and get their night horses and eat supper. So that night they went on guard as the time came, and next morning began to drive northward. We had some pleasant weather, and in a few days reached the North Platte river.

We had but little trouble in getting our cattle across, and next day moved one day's travel north of this river. Me and Arney went hunting, and killed a deer and a black wolf. When we got back Allen and Mason had a fight. They had gotten into a dispute about the negroes being freed, and one said they should never have been freed. During the conversation Allen said Mason called him a liar in a roundabout way. Mason said, "You are a liar if you say so." So Allen jumped at him, and hit him in the face. So Mason, in return, gave him one in the eye, and he went to the ground. Mason jumped on him and was preparing to bruise him, but was pulled off. So the fight ended.

When we came in Allen had a black eye. The fellow with me was a great one to laugh and ask questions. He was the first to notice his eye, and said, "You have been in a fight, have you? Who with – the negro cook?" Allen would not talk. "Say, cook, did you black Allen's eye?"

"No, sir, I don't black white people's eyes. All this negro fights is the black people."

"Who did this, anyway?"

"Mass Allen and Mason got to talking, and I was a cooking, and this negro looked around and both was on top of one another."

"Who blacked his eye?"

"Don't know, dis child would look no more, afraid they might want get hold of me."

"Who got the best of it?"

"Dis negro don't know. I would not look but once."

We all ate dinner and the boys relieved those on day herd, and we moved a short ways and camped for the night.

Chapter 40

WE CROSS INTO DAKOTA, CLOSE TO WHERE THE BURLINGTON AND MISSOURI RIVER RAILROAD LEAVES DAKOTA AND GOES INTO WYOMING. WE ARRIVE AT THE LYNCH RANCH. ME AND LYNCH AND ALSO MILLS GO HUNTING IN THE BLACK HILLS.

Next morning we saddled up and moved northward, and pretty soon crossed into Dakota. On the line where the Missouri River Railroad crosses was a pretty country. Lynch came to us next day at dinner. He was proud of his cattle as they were so fat and pretty. Next morning I was up toward the lead of the cattle while driving. I saw how nice they were getting along. Up rode a Sioux warrior and a negro, and stopped the cattle in the lead. I came on up and told them to get out of the way for we wanted the cattle to travel. The negro was the speaker and said, "We want a beef and when that is given to us we will get out of the way." He said they would let us go on. Said, "Squaws and bucks want beef. Heep hungry for beef." They had no more than got out the last word when I jumped off my horse with my Winchester rifle, and, calling them every name I could think of, and telling them if they did not get from in front of those cattle, I would give their squaws and bucks lead to eat instead of beef. They went off in a gallop over the hill.

Lynch came up about this time, and I told him all about the trouble. He said, "There are about five hundred camped below here. I wish you would have given them one, for they will be back and get what they want, if they have to kill us all to get it. Next time they come we will let them have what they want, and you had better tell them, so they will be in a good humor with you." Me and Lynch rode on together and talked. All at once we saw about seventy-five Sioux Indians coming toward us. We rode on as before. They said, "We want some beeves." I told them to go in and get what they wanted. Instead of getting out one they took three, and went on their way. I suppose they had a feast, but we had to give them up just the same.

After they were gone, the pointers threw them on the trail, and we began to drift northward again. In a few days we were at Lynch's ranch in the Black Hills, or at the edge of the hills called by some the Black Hills. On counting the cattle found we had lost but a small number. We turned them loose, and Lynch's men kept a watch over them, we were through with them, and I was glad of it. After turning them loose Lynch, me, and Mills went hunting, and killed three big black deer. They were twice as large as the red deer. The next thing was so funny. Me and Mills were shooting a silver tip bear, which rushed for Mills. Me and Lynch shot the bear, who was still after Mills, who was yelling at every step for us to shoot the negro-looking brute, as he did not have time. Me and Lynch put so much lead in him he became weak and fell on his face. Mills kept on running, we could hardly get him stopped, and when he did he said he was ready to go back to the ranch, for he had had enough of hunting for that day. We had a great laugh over it. We then started back and ran on three small black bears eating berries. We shot and killed them all, and then went on to camp and told the boys about the bear getting after Mills. "Yes," said Mills, "he never caught me either, that was the pretty part of it."

Next day we began to load our chuck wagon with something to eat, and made preparations to start to New Mexico. Everything was ready that night. We put the guards around our horses so they would be there next morning. The ones on last guard aroused us for breakfast, after which we caught our horses and were ready to start for the

Pecos Valley. Lynch tried to get me to stay with him, but I said, "No, by winter time I am going to be in New York city if I am living." So we all rode off on our long intended trip home.

Chapter 41

ON OUR WAY TO THE PECOS VALLEY OF NEW MEXICO, NEVER TO SEE THE NORTHERN COUNTRY AGAIN. MILLS WHIPS A GAMBLER AT CHEYENNE, WYOMING.

We traveled on southward and reached a small town on the Fremont, Elkhorn and Missouri Valley Railroad. The name of this small place was Harrison. We traveled on, and in a few days reached Cheyenne, Wyoming. Here we stopped a day or so. The boys put in most of their time playing cards and gambling.

The last day we were there Mills whipped a smart gambler. The cause of this trouble was, some of my men were playing poker with this gambler, and it was the gambler's deal. While dealing he took a card from the bottom instead of the top. Mills saw him do this and jumping, grabbed him by the collar and shook him around over the room, and kicked him awhile. He said, "I will learn you how to cheat us." By the time Mills had gotten through kicking him, the boys had taken all the money off the table and put it in their pockets and had passed out. The money amounted to over a thousand dollars. Mills did the same, and was soon at the camp. The gambler never did get a cent of the money. He never tried, I don't suppose.

We traveled on and came to Denver, Colorado, and camped close for the night. That night we went to a ball, and what a fine time we had. Me and Johnson were on the floor over half the time, dancing round and square sets. We then traveled on and soon came close to Pike's Peak. It was pretty to look at, it was so high. It was above the clouds. Colorado Springs is a pretty place, and is noted for a health resort and Pike's Peak.

From here we went on south and came to a town called Pueblo and stayed here one night. The boys went to another ball, but I did not go out. We still went on south and came to a town in Colorado by the name of Trinidad. I went to a ball at this place. We traveled on south and came to a town in the Panhandle by the name of Tascosa. It was located on the Canadian river. Next morning the boys went by and with their revolvers and guns and shot up the town. They did not like the people of this town, as one of my men had trouble here before. The place where it happened was at a ball.

We went on until we came to Fort Sumner, New Mexico, and learned that the kid had made his escape, after killing his two guards. When I got to the ranch Dixon told me all about it. So I will tell about it in the coming pages. We stayed at Sumner one night and from here went on to the Dixon ranch, arriving on the second day of September, 1881.

Chapter 42

BILLY THE KID MAKES HIS ESCAPE AFTER KILLING HIS TWO GUARDS. THEN GOES TO FORT SUMNER AND IS KILLED DURING THE SUMMER BY PAT GARRET, SHERIFF OF LINCOLN COUNTY.

Getting to the Dixon ranch we found everything all right. Dixon was proud to see us, and we told him about our trip to the Black Hills and that we lost but few cattle.

Dixon told us all about the kid's escape from Lincoln, after he had been sentenced to be hanged in April, by the judge of Don Ana county. He was taken by Garret and placed at Lincoln, Garret used a room over his office to keep the kid in, and had two men guard him. These men were Ollinger and Bell. The kid hated these men, having fought against each other during the Lincoln County War. Garret had a lot of other prisoners, who had given themselves up for protection. A lot of Tularosa Mexicans were after them. They had one fight and killed several Mexicans, and gave up for protection only. They were allowed to wear their revolvers, as there was danger of them being killed.

Sheriff Garret was forced to make a trip to White Oaks on business, and while making preparations to go, he told Ollinger and Bell to watch the kid closely, as he had but a few days to live and might try to escape. Ollinger said, "We will watch him like a goat." He then went and got his double-barrel shotgun and put a lot of buckshot in it, and said, "The one who gets this will feel it." The kid said, "You may get all of that."

Garret left next day for the Oaks, and when dinner time came Ollinger took the armed prisoners over to dinner, leaving Bell to guard the kid. The kid said after Ollinger took the armed prisoners over to dinner, Bell became interested in a paper, so he slipped one of the handcuffs off, and said he could have done it before if the right chance had come. As soon as he did this he jumped at Bell, using the handcuff as a weapon. Bell looked up from his newspaper and came very near fainting. He started downstairs after receiving a stunning blow on his head from the handcuffs. The kid reached forward and pulled his revolver. He had made no effort to draw it. Bell fell dead out in the yards with a bullet hole through his body.

After the kid had killed Bell he hobbled to the room where Ollinger had placed the gun he had loaded for him, and waited at an open window for Ollinger to return. Ollinger, on hearing the shooting, came in on a run, thinking it meant the kid's death. When he came in view of the window where the kid was waiting for him, the kid said, "Hello, Robert." When he looked up the kid emptied one barrel of the buckshot into his body. The kid, having obtained all the fire arms needed, which was two forty-five revolvers and a Winchester, went out and emptied the other barrel into Ollinger's body. Breaking the gun he threw it at the body and ordered the county clerk's horse, which he owned once. He then ordered his shackles filed off, which was done at double quick time. After doing this he got on the horse and rode westward and dashed out of sight.

When Garret returned from White Oaks he was sorry to learn of his two men being killed. He never made any hunt for the kid until he got a letter from a fellow at Fort Sumner saying the kid was making his home in that country.

Garret and two other men went to that part of the country. The men who went with him were strangers to that part. Garret stopped seven miles above at a running stream called Sunny-Side. He then sent one of his men to Sumner to see if he could find out anything. He came back soon and said there was no news. So Garret and his men went to Pete Maxwell's to see if he could find out anything from him. It was dark and Maxwell was asleep, so he woke him, and they began to talk. While this was going on the kid came in from the hills, and read the newspapers in the cook-room. Dropping his paper he told the cook to get him something to eat, for he was hungry. The Mexican cook said, "There is no meat in the house." He said, "I will have Maxwell get me some." So getting the butcher knife he started for Maxwell's room, and, seeing the men out on the grass, and not knowing who they were, asked twice in Mexican. They thought it was the Mexican peon and would not answer him. The kid walked in Maxwell's room and asked, "Pete, who is that out yonder?" Maxwell would not answer. The kid backed off and the light of the window was shining on him. Pete Maxwell said, "That is him, Garret." Garret fired and the first shot hit the kid's heart, and the next went in the ceiling, above their heads. The kid fell and took out his revolver. They say if his heart would have beat again he would have killed Garret. All ran out and would not come back again.

Maxwell's half-sister went in and found him dead. She was in love with the kid, and mourned over his grave many a time. The kid was buried the next day. Well, this is all the information I received, so I will write no more on this subject.

Chapter 43

THE LAST DAYS IN THE PECOS VALLEY OF NEW MEXICO. I GO TO PECOS CITY AND TAKE THE TRAIN FOR NEW YORK CITY.

After staying at the ranch a couple of days and seeing the boys ride wild horses, I began to think of leaving. One Mississippi boy thought he could ride a wild horse fine, but they would get him all over their backs and then throw him off. I began to get all my things together to leave. Dixon wanted me to stay, but I said, "I am going to see my loved one." He said, "Marry and come back and run my ranch." I said, "No, I am going to live with father the rest of the time."

So Dixon had me ride in his buggy and had a buckboard and three men go along. So we started, and had not gone far before the wind rose and the white dust from Salt creek looked like flour in the air. We traveled on but I will say no more about the journey.

We arrived at Pecos City all right. I boarded a Texas and Pacific train for Texarkana. I got to this place all O.K. I changed cars, and got on the St. Louis, Iron Mountain and Southern for St. Louis. We ran on this train until we came to Malvern, Arkansas. Here we had to stop one day on account of there being something wrong with the track.

I had a nice time there at Malvern. There was so many nice people there at that time. I went to a ball there and danced only squares, for there was no round dancing. The Arkansas girls were very pretty. You could hardly get the boys to make you acquainted and they said people never did such in that country. One boy told me to get a partner. I told him I wanted an introduction, but he said no. It was some time before I got started. But I soon put on my gall and pinned back my ears and went flying at them. About one-thirty I began to get sleepy, and went to the hotel to bed. The next morning I talked to a girl at the hotel until the train came. I boarded her for St. Louis. I had a nice run of it, and arrived all O.K.

I stopped here one day and tried to find out where Tom was. After some search I found a man who was acquainted with him. He told me Tom was very wealthy and had bought a dry goods house, and made twice his money on that. He said every trade was something similar. I told him I was proud to hear Tom was doing so well. He said Tom had a baby girl at his house, and he thinks it is the finest one living. It can walk around. I did not see Tom, for I did not want to talk of the past.

I then got on the Baltimore and Ohio Southwestern for New York city. Arriving there I prowled around the city, and made inquiries about Mr. Hale. I acted as if I were a friend of his. At a dry goods house I made inquiries and one of the clerks said he was well acquainted with Mr. Hale. He said the old man was rich enough, and wished he had to starve until he gave him part of it, and said Hale bought some real estate and made twice the amount invested. He said it would beat a Jew how he made money, and never worked either. He asked, "Are you acquainted with him?"

I said, "I knew him when I was small. I don't know whether he would recognize me or not."

I also asked him if Hale was married. He said, "Yes, and has the prettiest stepdaughter."

"Does she want to marry?"

He said, "No, I think she is waiting for the old man's son, with whom she is smitten." He also said if a man were to get her he would get a nice lot of money.

I said, "I may go down and see Hale."

I then walked off and put on my best clothes, to go and see father and his children. I walked around until night, and went to my father's house. On arriving at the house I met a negro. I asked him if a man by the name of Hale lived there. He said yes and asked me if I wished to see him and I told him I did. The negro said he would return in a moment when he told Mr. Hale a man wished to see him.

Chapter 44

WE ARE ALL TOGETHER AGAIN, AND FATHER IS HAPPY I AM AT HOME.

The negro came back soon and said, "Here is the man that wants to see you."

"Well," said father, "you have come home again. Come in and see the people." So we went in. There was the girl and her mother. And what a glad meeting it was.

They said, "Why did you not tell us when you were going to be here." I told them I wanted to take them by surprise. So we talked until late and father said it was time to retire. The waiter woke me next morning for breakfast.

After preparing and fixing my clothes as nicely as possible the negro opened the door and said, "Mass Hale and the other people wait in the sitting room for you." I then went in and we went to breakfast. After the meal was over we went to the sitting room. Father told me about the money he had invested, and what a great income it brought, and also said, "I am so glad you have come home so you can manage it for me."

Grace asked me if I was going to stay, or go to the West again. I told her for the present I was thinking of going west no more.

Father's wife said she would give a fine supper, and make me acquainted with the people. I told them for the present I had no desire to form a lot of acquaintances; that it had been so long since I had been with up-to-date people it would scare me to go where the crowd was too large. If they wore a couple of revolvers and a double-edge Mexican knife I would feel at home. Grace said, "Listen at him, will you?"

"Well," said father, "we will have no supper, as it will be of no benefit to us in any way, and will be so wearisome." He said, "If you will agree and go with us we will sell everything and go across the waters to England to live." I told him I was in the notion to do anything they wanted me to.

Now I am not going to tell the names of property and the locations, nor give any light on the past, for several reasons, which I will not give. Father said, "A certain hotel brings me in about a thousand a year, and I will sell this and you can have the money if you still live with us, and besides it does not pay enough interest for the amount of money invested." He said, "There is a rich Englishman who wants to buy our property, and change its name."

I said I was willing to do all of this, if I did not change my notion. He said, "Good, I want to go to a new place, and the first thing is to go to Buffalo and sell a dry goods house I purchased there. It is rented by a Jew, by the name of Sam Imy, who is crazy to buy it. It is wearisome for he writes me a letter every week, saying he would like to purchase it." And father said, "Me and you will go in a few days and dispose of that property, and when we sell everything we will cross the water."

This is not all the conversation we had, but I will give only what is required for an explanation. We had been talking and the time seemed so short that we were surprised to hear the dinner bell ring. We then went to dinner, and father was talking all the while. He said, "I was happy when I left the wild countries. How about you and those other boys? It would not have surprised me the way you all were doing, to hear you had been killed any time."

Dinner was over and Grace said, "Come and look at the pretty flowers. I have such a nice lot of them."

Father said, "Don't stay long, as I want all the news from that western country."

So me and Grace went to the flower house and looked at the flowers, and talked. In a short while we took seats as there were a couple of chairs in the flower house. Grace said, "I thought you never were coming back to see us again."

I said, "I would have been here sooner but you made the said time so long." I will give as little of this love affair as I can, as I do not like to write on such.

Chapter 45

I Get Married and We Dispose of the Property, and Make Preparations to Go to England.

I asked, "Is our time up to get married?"

She said, "It is."

I said again, "When will it be?"

Grace said, "Any time suits me, let us marry at once. In two days, that will be short enough."

I said, "All right."

We sat and talked in the flower house until late. It was getting supper time so we went to our father's and mother's room. Father said, "I see you never stayed long. I could hardly pass off the time while you all were gone. Sit down, I want to talk to you some before supper."

Grace said, "We are going to get married."

"Yes," father said, "Sit down. When do you all want to marry?"

Grace said, "In two days." Father said he did not care if we married in two minutes.

"What about that New Mexico country, what do they do there, run cattle?"

I said, "The cowboys run cattle, fight, drink, gamble, and steal. It is a bad country to live in."

"How is that man you went to that country with?"

"He is doing well, and was a fine man."

"What is his name?"

I said, "Dixon."

Just then father left the room, and we three were left in the room. Mother told me father would be contented since I came home. Then me and Grace commenced to talk to her about us going by one name. Her mother said it would please her well. Father came in the room, and at that moment the bell rang for supper.

After supper was over me and Grace talked and played games until late. Next morning I was up when the negro came to arouse me. When I went to the sitting room I found them all waiting for me. So we all went to breakfast. It was not long before father and mother had a wedding at their place, and the ones that got married were me and Grace.

Soon after, me and father went to Buffalo to sell that property I was speaking of. So Grace and her mother went along also. We began to make preparations to take what we needed.

I got a letter from Pecos City, wanting to know if I arrived home all right, and if I ever figured on coming to New Mexico again. I wrote and told him the trip was wearisome, but I had arrived all right; that I had married and what a pretty girl married me. In my letter I told him, if he could come to New York I would get my woman to find one equally as pretty. Dixon said the cattle business was pretty good, but some time he was going to quit this life. I may write some more on the western life, but don't think I will.

Me, father, and the women started for Buffalo and had a nice trip of it. We sold this property for a nice lot of money, and after father called on another man, and collected some money due, we went back to our home.

We stayed at home quite a while before we began to sell any more of the property. I received another letter from Dixon, who said a man was on a deal with him and that he might be in that country but a few days. "I will write and tell you, so you can come to see me if I don't sell." He also said the sheep were causing trouble. They were coming in great herds from the mountains.

Our next sale was a hotel, which gave us a nice sum of money. It was enough to make some people think they were rich. It was not long before all the property was sold and we were in fine circumstances, and would continue so if we were careful and made no bad investments.

We were about ready to go to England. Father said there was another man he wished to see before leaving. While waiting for father, me and Grace would put in the time driving and walking around. Father soon saw his man and got everything fixed up. Then father had to go to Baltimore. A man owed him some money and father, having too much confidence in him, never made him give any security, so he did not have to pay father unless he wanted to. The fellow, hearing father was going to leave the country, offered to pay if he would come down. So I wrote him a nice letter and told him father would be down at once. Father went and collected the ten thousand without any trouble, and returned on the next train.

Chapter 46

THE TRIP TO ENGLAND GIVEN UP. I TALK FATHER IN THE NOTION NOT TO GO.

The next day we were prepared to go, and I had a long talk with father. I had gotten out of the notion. I told father I did not think I would ever be satisfied in that country, for it was nothing but towns and settlements. There were so many people living on the farms it would look like towns in the country, and I told him I could not stand to cross the ocean, as the ship might go down and there was lots of danger.

He got mad and said, "I would just as soon travel on the ocean as on one of those passenger trains, and there is less danger on a vessel. He said he did not care whether I went or not, so the women were to decide. Grace said they would not leave one another, so father was over his mad spell by morning and said he would go where I wanted to live, as he wanted to be with his only boy and step-daughter, whom he thought so much of. He said, "I may not be long here on this earth, and I want to be satisfied. You all have a talk and decide where you wish to go, as we have sold and I am going to change places."

So we all had a talk and said we would take a pleasure trip westward. We went to St. Louis, and after staying here several days, went to Denver, Colorado. We enjoyed ourselves traveling around. We visited Pike's Peak, and this was a great sight for the women. Father said he liked the country so much better. I went on a hunt in the mountains, and killed a bear and two large black deer. Father said he liked the West so well he was glad we did not go the other route. I went on another hunt, which lasted several days, and killed a lot of animals. Everyone enjoyed themselves.

I came back after this hunt, and we all went up to Utah, and looked at that country. It was wonderful to see the Mormon Temple at Salt Lake City. And the Mormons, what a curious people. They may change later. Oh, I will say there is plenty of room for it. I did not like the Mormon country. They say a while before these were the meanest people under the sun. Of course I did not know, and I did not want any experience to know. I began to get tired of this country, and asked my people when they would be ready to go. They all said they had been ready a long time.

We went back to Denver and from there to Las Vegas, New Mexico, and after staying here quite a while we then went on to San Antonio, which is in Texas. We went over to the Mexican side, so the women could see the natives. They were terribly thick, very few white people living there. I went back in the cattle trade after visiting the country. I will not say where I am located, it being between San Antonio and the Panhandle of Texas. Whereabout I will not say. Cattle trade was my delight. Grace said there could be no better life than the ranch life, and said she believed anyone would live longer. The cattle were so pretty.

Father and mother said they would not make their home with us all the while, as they would visit and pass off the time. So I and the boys went to looking after the cattle, which seemed to be well satisfied after we had branded them. Father and mother would drive out and look at them every once in a while, and Grace would take her horseback rides. She thought there was nothing could pass off the time any better. Father and mother said they liked this life, but would soon go north again on pleasure trips.

The cattle did well, but we had trouble with mustang horses, which means wild horses. These horses would come to ours and take them off, and ours would want to stay with them on account of being young colts. They gave us so much trouble. We rode out with our rifles and killed a lot of them. They were pretty wild, but we managed to run on them and kill some of them. One time we hid at a watering place and killed a lot of them while they were coming in to water.

We went on a hunting expedition, and every time we saw any of these horses, we would shoot at them. One of the boys ran on one large horse and roped him. He fought like a tiger, and the man came very near getting hurt. The animal was so unruly, he was forced to turn him loose. He shot him twice, it taking effect. So he got his fine rope back again which was around the horse's neck.

Chapter 47

THE COWBOYS HAVE A FIGHT WITH SOME MEXICAN WILD HORSE HUNT-ERS.

I went on back to the ranch, and the boys kept on hunting wild horses. A lot of Mexicans caught these horses to use, and there were some Mexicans who had caught a lot of these animals, and had them about under control. My men ran into their horses and shot at them and ran their horses off. So the Mexicans and the boys had a fight with their revolvers and rifles. One of the boys was shot. All the horses the Mexicans rode were killed, nine in number. There was no trouble after this. I rode over and saw the Mexicans, and paid them for the horses the boys had run off and killed. They had on their war paint, but I made everything satisfactory with them. They then left this part and went to another to hunt horses. I told the boys not to treat them that way any more, as they had the advantage of them, the Mexicans being quite a ways from their country, and were following this for a living.

The boys kept on hunting the wild horses until they killed them all. The Mexicans hated the boys after this and waited their chance.

Tom Lyle's men went on a gambling trip, and one night four of them were murdered. Some of these Mexicans were supposed to have done this. I don't suppose they got the men they wanted. My men were careful after this, as they were afraid of a surprise. A Mexican will kill a white man, any time he can get a chance, if the man's back is to him. Some Mexicans came in Lyle's range but his men ran them out, so no more came in, as they were afraid.

Chapter 48

A TRIP TO LAS VEGAS, NEW MEXICO, WITH FATHER AND MOTHER, WHO ARE ON A TRIP TO DENVER, COLORADO.

Mother and father said they were going to leave the ranch for a while, and did not know how long they were going to be gone. They said they were going to Denver and wanted me and Grace to go as far as Las Vegas with them. We made our trip all right, and while at Las Vegas ran on Bob Anson, who was an old acquaintance of mine. He was with us when us and the Smith boys ragged with the Mexicans, in the southern part. He said after we left, the Mexicans were glad. Still, they would like to have burned us. And he said, "After you five left, there were about four hundred came over, and, after looking around, went back to Old Mexico. So it was a good thing you boys left that country." He also said there was no more trouble after this, that he believed we made them believe it was danger-ous to molest the white man. He said Scott was worth any amount of money. And said that other girl was around Matamoros. We stayed at Las

Vegas several days, until mother and father went on to Denver. Then we went back to the ranch. The cowboys were taking good care of the cattle, and were well satisfied. What pleased me was the cattle. Getting so fat.

Grace enjoyed the life in the West, but said she did not think we ought to stay there all the time, as we might get weary, and become dissatisfied. She said some time we had better take pleasure trips east. I told her any time she wished to go I was ready, as I wanted to keep and have everything pleasant for her.

We had not been home long before we received a letter from father and mother saying they wanted us to meet them at Las Vegas, so they could come back to the ranch. They said the people were so unsocial they were coming back to the ranch. We met them at Las Vegas, New Mexico.

I went around town and had a talk with the cattlemen. Some were from Texas and said they were crowded pretty bad by settlers. They said farmers were coming in raising good crops, and believed they were going to stay, and asked me what I thought about it. I said, "Us cowmen and cowboys helped drive out the Indians, so there was no room for them, and then the farmers come and there is not enough range for our cattle, so we will have to go as the Indian did. It is my belief the time will come when there will be but a few Indians left, and the large cattleman will be five hundred times more scarce."

Printed in the United States
4954

9 781589 761001